Parenting Teenage Girls

10 Key Topics to Discuss With Your Teenage Daughter in Today's World

Rebecca Flag - Dawn Publishing House

Parenting Teenage Girls

10 Key Topics to Discuss With Your
Teenage Daughter in Today's World

Rebecca Hay, Dawn Publishing House

© Copyright 2022 - All rights reserved.

The content contained within this book may not be reproduced, duplicated or transmitted without direct written permission from the author or the publisher.

Under no circumstances will any blame or legal responsibility be held against the publisher, or author, for any damages, reparation, or monetary loss due to the information contained within this book, either directly or indirectly.

Legal Notice:

This book is copyright protected. It is only for personal use. You cannot amend, distribute, sell, use, quote or paraphrase any part, or the content within this book, without the consent of the author or publisher.

Disclaimer Notice:

Please note the information contained within this document is for educational and entertainment purposes only. All effort has been executed to present accurate, up to date, reliable, complete information. No warranties of any kind are declared or implied. Readers acknowledge that the author is not engaged in the rendering of legal, financial, medical or professional advice. The content within this book has been derived from various sources. Please consult a licensed professional before attempting any techniques outlined in this book.

By reading this document, the reader agrees that under no circumstances is the author responsible for any losses, direct or indirect, that are incurred as a result of the use of the information contained within this document, including, but not limited to, errors, omissions, or inaccuracies.

Table of Contents

INTRODUCTION 1

CHAPTER 1: PUBERTY AND THE CHANGES THAT COME WITH IT 5

TALKING TO YOUR TEENAGE DAUGHTER ABOUT PUBERTY 5
    Puberty In Girls (Physical Changes) 6
    When Is the Right Time To Talk About Puberty? 11
    Tips To Help You Start a Puberty Conversation With Your Teenage Daughter 13
    In Closing 17

CHAPTER 2: SEX, AND OTHER KINDS OF PHYSICAL INTIMACY 19

TALKING TO YOUR TEENAGE DAUGHTER ABOUT SEX 19
    When is The Right Time to Talk About Sex? 20
    Understanding the Signs 22
    The Actual Conversation 25
    Why Sex at a Young Age isn't a Good Idea 28
    In Closing 32

CHAPTER 3: PEER PRESSURE AND ITS CONSEQUENCES 35

HOW PEER PRESSURE AFFECTS A TEENAGE GIRL'S LIFE 35
    What Is Peer Pressure? 36
    The Difference between Positive and Negative Influence From Peers 38
    Being Pressured by Parents and Family Members 39
    Strategies You Could Share with Your Child to Cope With Peer Pressure 40
    In Closing 44

CHAPTER 4: TEENAGE DEPRESSION 45

DEPRESSION AND ANXIETY IN ADOLESCENCE 45
    Why is Depression Common Among Teenagers? 47
    Signs Of Depression in Teenagers 51
    How are Teenagers Diagnosed With Depression? 57
    What are The Warning Signs that Indicate Your Teenager is Headed for Suicide? 59
    Speaking to Your Teenager About Suicide 62
    What Should You Do if Your Teenager is Suicidal? 65
    In Closing 68

CHAPTER 5: THE IMPORTANCE OF DECISION-MAKING **69**

TEACHING YOUR CHILD HOW TO MAKE GOOD CHOICES IN LIFE 69
   Why Can't Teenagers Make Good Choices? 70
   Consequences Of Bad Decision-Making 72
   Good Decision-Making Tips for You to Share With Your Teenager 76
   In Closing 77

CHAPTER 6: THE TOXIC SOCIAL CULTURE OF THE WORLD TODAY **79**

PREPARING YOUR TEENAGER TO FACE THE WORLD 79
   Youth Culture Today 80
   In Closing 83

CHAPTER 7: THE IMPORTANCE OF SELF-RESPECT AND CONFIDENCE IN ADOLESCENCE **85**

TEACHING YOUR DAUGHTER HOW TO BE CONFIDENT AND RESPECTFUL. 85
   What is Self-Confidence, and What is Meant By Self-Respect? 86
   How to Overcome Shame and Embarrassment 90
   How You Can Help Build Self-Confidence in Your Teenager 92
   In Closing 95

CHAPTER 8: SPIRITUALITY AND BELIEFS **97**

TALKING TO YOUR TEENAGER ABOUT THEIR SPIRITUALITY 97
   Adolescence and Spirituality 98
   Ways that You Can Help Your Teenager Get Closer to God 100
   In Closing 102

CHAPTER 9: GOALS AND EDUCATION **103**

TALKING TO YOUR TEENAGER ABOUT GOALS AND THE IMPORTANCE OF EDUCATION 103
   The Importance of Being Educated and Ambitious as a Young Woman ... 104
   Why are Teenagers Unambitious? 107
   Why is Goal-Setting Important? 109
   In Closing 112

CHAPTER 10: CONFLICT MANAGEMENT **113**

TALKING TO YOUR TEENAGER ABOUT MANAGING CONFLICT IN A HEALTHY WAY 113
   Why are Teenagers Always Involved in Conflict? 114
   How Will Poor Conflict Management Impact a Teenager's Life? 116
   Ways Your Teenager Can Manage Conflict 118
   In Closing 120

CONCLUSION **121**

REFERENCES **123**
　Image References 125

Introduction

Parenting is one of the toughest jobs on the planet. The only thing tougher than that is parenting teenage girls. Oh yes, you heard me right! Teenage girls are in a league of their own. They are moody, opinionated, fun-loving individuals who are going through the most confusing and life-changing phase in their lives. It's incredibly hard for them to understand the entire process of becoming an adult woman. Teenage girls heavily depend on the guidance of their parents, but sometimes it can be a confusing time for the parents as well. Such was the situation with mother and daughter, Holly and Nelsie. Holly was a hardworking mom with three beautiful children. One of those children was a 15-year-old teenage girl named Nelsie. Nelsie had been going through a lot of stuff in her life, with the divorce of her parents and starting out a new year at a new school. She had left all of her old friends behind, and she was entering a new phase in her life.

With all the new adjustments she had to get used to, Nelsie was also going through puberty. She was experiencing changes to her body that were completely new to her. Nelsie and her mom didn't have a close relationship, as her mom had been going through a messy divorce. Her attention was not on Nelsie at this moment because she had to worry about finding a new job, so she could support her family. Nelsie didn't have anyone else to talk to. Her younger siblings were 8-year-old twin boys, and she just recently moved to a new city. She felt alone and confused, and she held a lot of anger towards her father and mother inside her. They were supposed to be helping her understand this phase she was going through. Instead, they were more focused on themselves, constantly fighting and ignoring their children.

Nelsie didn't understand what pain her parents were in because of their divorce. Yes, her feelings were valid, but she couldn't see past them in order to understand where her parents were coming from. This strained the relationship she shared with her mom, and she kept all her feelings and troubles to herself. Holly wanted to connect with her daughter, but she felt closed off and unwanted because Nelsie had built up a wall to keep her mother out. There was so much about life that Holly wanted to teach Nelsie. She wanted to prepare her daughter to face the world, so she wouldn't make the same mistakes that she did when she was younger. Nelsie wanted that guidance and support from her mother, but she wouldn't allow herself to open up and become vulnerable around her. She was afraid of being hurt because she thought her mother wouldn't always be around to help her.

Misunderstandings are common between parents and teenagers these days. We all like to create our own view on things, and we refuse to look at things from another angle. There are always two sides to every story—which both parents and their children have to understand. For teenage girls, their mothers are the most important support system they look at during puberty. However, not everyone is fortunate enough to have both parents in their lives. There are so many teenage girls out there who don't have their moms around to help them answer questions about the changes that are taking place in their body. It's hard to talk to your dad about these things. It can seem awkward and uncomfortable. These teenage girls need a motherly figure in their lives, such as a grandmother, aunt, or big sister, to help them through it.

Dads can prove to be the support system that their teenage daughters need, but they have to understand the process in order for them to answer all the questions and concerns that their teenage daughters might have. This book is going to help both moms and dads learn how to talk to their teenage daughters about important aspects of life. If you are a parent who is confused and at your wits' end about what you should talk to your teenage daughter about, then you have chosen the right book to help you. We are going to show you how to open up and connect more with your child. This will make the whole process a lot easier to go through. So get ready to become the best parent your teenager could ever hope for! Be open, be willing, and be kind throughout this journey, and you will see a change in your relationship with your daughter.

Chapter 1:
Puberty and the Changes That Come With It

Talking to Your Teenage Daughter About Puberty

Puberty is the most important time in a girl's life. This is the crucial phase in which she learns more about herself as she grows and

develops into a young woman. It's exciting to leave behind childhood days and embrace the new chapter of life, but it can also be exceptionally frightening and confounding. There will be a lot of changes that a girl will experience during puberty. Keep in mind that these changes that occur to her body will be uncomfortable, and she will have a hard time warming up to these changes. Your teenage daughter will need your guidance the most because you have been through this phase in your life before. She will expect you to have all the answers, but if we're being realistic, you probably wouldn't know what to say to her. In this chapter, we are going to help you learn about the physical and emotional changes that puberty will bring. This will enable you to become more understanding towards your daughter, and it will prepare you to answer all of her questions that are related to puberty.

Puberty In Girls (Physical Changes)

Puberty begins during the last stages of childhood, between the ages of eight and thirteen. It happens in both boys and girls. The most obvious changes that occur during puberty are the physical aspects, such as height, weight, facial features, voice changes, and the genitals. There are several factors that come into play which will determine when a girl will start puberty. Factors such as race, genetics, ethnicity, and body weight will determine when a teenage girl will start going through puberty. There is no exact time or exact age for puberty to kick in. It happens when the time is right. Girls experience puberty a lot more differently than boys do. The complete process can be very uncomfortable and overwhelming for girls. In this section, we will look at the distinct changes that take place during puberty in more detail. The more you open yourself up to learning about these changes as a parent, the more confidence you will have to talk to your teenage daughter about them. Below, we look at some of the physical changes that occur during puberty.

Changes In Breasts

One of the first signs of puberty in teenage girls is the appearance of breast buds. Breast buds appear just beneath the nipples, and they feel like two small lumps of tissue. Depending on the race, these changes will appear around 8-years-old for Blacks and Hispanics, and if you are White or Asian, these changes will appear at around nine or ten years old. Race and ethnicity play an enormous factor in puberty, and being a heavier weight will cause puberty to start earlier than expected. Now, it takes a while before the breasts can grow into their full size, and this can be uncomfortable for a lot of teenage girls. They could also be insecure about one breast growing faster than the other, but this is completely normal and a part of the process.

While the breasts are growing, it would be painful and most girls prefer to wear padded bras to help with the sensitivity. Your teenage daughter will have a lot of questions regarding their growing breasts. Help your teen daughter understand that their growing breasts are their body's way of preparing them to nurture a baby. This has everything to do with the biology of a woman and is the purpose behind having breasts.

Be straightforward and open to help your teen understand why these changes are happening now.

Menstrual Cycle (Periods) and Vaginal Discharge

This is one of the most significant changes a teenage girl will experience. Getting her period is a proud moment that is usually shared between mothers and daughters because it signifies that she is no longer a little girl, and she is on her way to becoming a woman. This is an internal change that brings about a lot of hormonal changes and mood swings. Your daughter would want to understand why she is getting her periods, and you have to explain this to her by being transparent and open. The main reason girls experience a menstrual cycle is that their body is preparing their ovaries and uterus to conceive and house a baby for nine months. When your daughter gets her period, it could scare her and find it confusing. The more educated you are about this, the more comfort you can offer her. Parents have to prepare themselves for the intense mood swings and change in behavior that comes with this additional aspect of their daughter's life.

Vaginal discharge is another important aspect that has to be discussed with your teenage daughter. There are different vaginal discharges that each shows whether the vagina is healthy. Discharge that is clear or whitish is healthy, however, discharge that is yellow or green, with a foul odor, shows an infection in the vagina. It would be incredibly difficult for a dad to have this conversation with his daughter, but we understand that sometimes a dad is all a teenager has. The best option would be to ask a nurse or teacher, preferably female, to explain the menstrual cycle and vaginal discharge to your daughter, as they would feel more comfortable speaking about this with a female. As a father, knowing what you can talk to your teenage daughter about, and what you can't, will make your conversations a lot simpler to navigate. For moms, these topics are not so difficult to talk to their daughters about, as they have a deeper understanding and first-hand experience.

Body Hair

The growth of body hair also occurs during the initial stages of puberty. Your daughter will notice a significant amount of hair growing under her arms, on her face, on her legs, and around the pubic area. Facial hair would appear on the chin and around the upper lip. This might be a good time to talk to your teenager about shaving and waxing to manage their hair growth. It's important that parents educate their daughters on what forms of hair removal are safe and best for their skin types. Some girls develop a rash after waxing or using hair removal creams. If your daughter's skin is sensitive, consider getting products that are free from harsh chemicals and fragrances. Your daughter shouldn't feel pressured to remove hair from their body unless they are 100% sure about it. Allow your daughter to express her concerns about hair removal as it can be a sensitive topic for a lot of girls who come from a Black background. Hair can be thicker and darker for girls of color, and this can make the removal process more difficult. Teach them about being hygienic and keeping themselves clean even if they decide they don't want to remove any hair from their body just yet.

Acne and Pimples

Acne, the number one reason so many teenagers lose their self-confidence. As hated as acne may be, there is nothing you can do to avoid it. There are things you can do to manage it and minimize the break-out's. Acne can be small, red, pus filled pimples that show up on your face, neck and forehead. Blackheads and white heads also accompany them. The main reason acne shows up during puberty is because of the changes in your teenager's hormones. These hormones cause the skin to produce more oils, which clogs the pores, along with dead skin cells and bacteria. The severity of their acne can affect your teenager's confidence. For some girls, their feelings about their acne had led to depression and anxiety. Encourage your teenager by explaining how acne is a part of adolescence and there are things that can be done to improve their break-out's. Using face wash, exfoliating every night before bed, and using a cream to keep the skin dry and oil free are all great ways to manage acne.

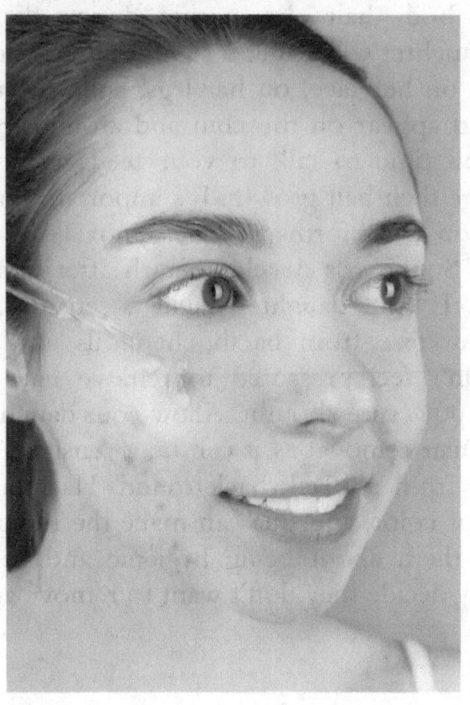

Body Odor

As the body develops during puberty, there are a lot of changes that will take place. One of these very noticeable changes is body odor. Now, body odor isn't only something that boys experience during puberty. Girls also experience changes in their body odor and this can make them feel insecure. Because of the excess oil production by their skin, when mixed with sweat, it can give off an unpleasant odor. Physical activity will cause the body to produce more sweat, so encourage your teenager to bathe at least twice a day after playing sports, or being involved in any other forms of physical activity. Using roll on and antiperspirant deodorant can help keep the unpleasant odors at bay. There is nothing to be ashamed of, as everyone sweats and it's a normal part of being human. Help your daughter understand that body odor can be managed by keeping yourself fresh.

Gaining or Losing Weight

Most girls lose a lot of baby fat during their teenage years—this is because of the changes in the body's metabolism and hormones. During childhood, your daughter would have gained some weight, but during adolescence, there will be a chance that most of the weight will fall off. However, this might not always be the case, as some kids maintain their overall stature throughout their teenage years and into adulthood. Some kids might gain weight during puberty built in their childhood, despite being small. It has a lot to do with genetics and hormones that are released during puberty. There is no sure way to tell how a girl's body will change during puberty and weight loss, or gain, is a normal part of this process. If your teenage daughter has gained weight, and she is feeling insecure about it, encourage her to eat healthy and lead an active lifestyle. Sometimes weight gain could be attributed to a medical condition like thyroid issues, so it would be a good idea to get a check-up done just to make sure all is well. Extreme weight loss could also show an underlying issue, such as an eating disorder. Parents have to be more vigilant and pay attention to how their teenager's body is changing. When something doesn't feel right, get your daughter checked out by a medical professional.

When Is the Right Time To Talk About Puberty?

There is no set time to have a discussion with your teenage daughter about puberty. Because every teenager is different, they will grow and develop at their own pace. Some girls wouldn't get their period until they're 12-years-old, others would start developing breasts when they're nine or 10-years-old. Knowing when to sit down and talk to your teenage daughter about these changes will be hard to determine. Most parents sit back and wait for their daughters to approach them with questions they might have when the time is right. This could work when the parents and children have a good relationship. However, most girls would feel ashamed to go to their parents and ask questions about these changes that are happening to them.

It all depends on how your personal relationship is with your daughter. If you have an open relationship where you feel comfortable talking about serious issues with your kids, then you can start addressing puberty as soon as your daughter becomes curious about the changes that are happening to her body. Speaking to a 10-year-old about puberty differs from speaking to a 13-year-old. Their level of understanding would differ, so it would be best to talk to your teenage daughter whenever they are ready. There are a few things you can do to determine whether it is the right time to talk to your teen.

Reassure Your Daughter

The best way to determine if your teenager is ready to talk about the changes that are happening to her body is to ask her if she's ready to talk. You can ask your daughter from time to time if she is doing okay or if she wants to talk to you about anything. It's that simple. Sometimes, your daughter might need some reassurance from you that shows you are a safe place for them to go to with their concerns. At the end of the day, it's important that you are both on the same page, so it doesn't become uncomfortable when you talk about puberty. Usually, parents are the last people teenagers want to open up and talk about these changes with. Helping them feel secure and safe is critical so they know they can come to you at any time.

Don't Be Pushy

As a parent, it's normal to feel nervous about having these conversations with your daughter, more so for mothers, rather than for fathers. Moms can sometimes become eager to speak to their daughters about all the changes that are going on in their body. However, it's important to understand where your teenager is coming from. Ask yourself whether your daughter is ready to talk about what is going on with her body. Remember, this can be an extremely uncomfortable time for her, so it's best that you hold these conversations until your daughter is comfortable. Don't force the topic and don't be pushy. It could backfire and cause your daughter to close herself up from you.

The Right Age

Puberty can start as early as 8-years-old and last until your daughter is 17-years-old. This is a long phase, and knowing when is the right age to bring up conversations about puberty can be difficult. Make sure that your daughter isn't too young when you are having these conversations with her because she might not understand. The right age would be around 15-years-old, your daughter's level of understanding would be higher, and she could make sense of the information you are giving her. It's important that she can comprehend what you are saying, and her interaction and participation in the conversation would be necessary. She wouldn't be able to interact with you if she couldn't understand what was being said.

Tips To Help You Start a Puberty Conversation With Your Teenage Daughter

Parents can be clueless when it comes to having a serious conversation with their teenagers about their body. Below, we have a few tips to help you start the conversation with your teenage daughter. These tips will help keep the conversation going and also help to avoid scaring your teenager off in the middle of talking. Even if you are talking to your daughter who hasn't fully become a teenager just yet, these tips will help you explain things without making it sound too complicated for them to understand.

Tips For Talking to Older Teenagers

Make Your Daughter Feel Comfortable

To help your teenager feel more comfortable, you could take your daughter out for lunch, away from other family members, where you could talk about things in private. Having other siblings, or other family members around, could make things uncomfortable for your daughter. You could have a fun spa day and treat your daughter to a facial or a pedicure. Spending quality time together would help your daughter feel more connected with you. This will help her open up and be receptive towards the things you will discuss with her. Older teenagers usually feel disconnected from their parents, and this will make them hesitant to share their feelings.

Questions and Answers Should be Short

Your teenager would already feel uncomfortable talking about these things with you. To make it less awkward, keep your questions and answers as short as possible. Keep in mind that your daughter will already have some knowledge about the changes that are happening to her body. Girls usually share this information with their friends first before talking to their parents about it. Most of the time, their understanding of puberty isn't entirely correct, so parents should ask their teenagers about what they know already. Ask in the most simple way possible, don't beat around the bush. Simple questions will help your teenager answer without hesitation. Prolonging the conversation with unnecessary questions will only make your teenager feel more uncomfortable.

Reassure Your Teenager When You Sense Hesitation

The only way you can keep the conversation going is by making your teenager feel comfortable. Whenever you sense your daughter is being hesitant when she wants to ask you a question or if she wants to share information with you, the best thing you can do at that moment is to reassure her. Tell her it is okay for her to be open with you about things, and that no one else has to know what they said. Encourage her to take her time and allow her to answer when she is ready. If she has questions that are uncomfortable for her to ask, you can try to offer an explanation without her having to say these things out loud. Try to pick up on the small clues she leaves when she is talking to you. Her body language and facial expressions will tell you how comfortable she is and when she needs reassurance.

Give Her Space

If your daughter doesn't want to have this conversation with you, allow her to take some time for herself. It might take a while for her to warm up to the idea of having a conversation with you about her body. Even if you are the mom, she might still feel uncomfortable or self-conscious of herself. If you are the dad, your daughter might not want to talk to you about the changes that are happening to her body. She would be more open about her emotions and feelings. Dad's should arrange for a female that is close to their daughters to have this conversation with her. As a parent, it can frustrate you when your child doesn't want to open up and let you in. But you have to respect their privacy and give them their space. She will eventually come to you in the future and ask for your advice and guidance. Make sure your relationship isn't affected because she needs space and allow yourself to be available for when she is ready to talk.

Tips For Talking to Younger Teenagers

Try Not to Look Uncomfortable

When talking to your younger teenagers, make sure you look confident, even if it means you have to pretend. If your child notices you are uncomfortable talking to them about puberty, then they will lose interest in the conversation and close themselves off. The more nervous you behave, the more embarrassed and uncomfortable your daughter can become. As a parent, show your child that it's okay to talk about these things and that there is nothing to be embarrassed about.

Keep The Conversation Sweet and Short

Since puberty is so sensitive and uncomfortable to talk about, try to keep the conversation short and to the point. You don't have to talk about things in much detail as long as your daughter gains an understanding of what is happening to her body during puberty. By talking too much about it, your teenager will lose their focus and become uninterested quickly.

Don't Act Like You Know It All

Parents can sometimes come across as being too obnoxious with their explanations. Especially when they are talking to their teenage daughters about important aspects of puberty. There's nothing teenagers hate more than having a parent who is more interested in knowing it all, rather than being genuine in their conversations. Show your daughter that you are engaged in this conversation because you genuinely want to help them. Parents should tone it down a little when having conversations with their children. Be more understanding and less judgmental.

Use Wise Examples When Explaining

It might surprise you at how much your daughter already knows about puberty and her body. Try not to use examples that insult the intelligence of your teenage daughter. In most cases, parents share a bit too much information that doesn't really have to be shared with their teenagers. It makes them feel uncomfortable and gives them the impression that you don't feel they are intelligent enough to figure most of it out on their own. Observe how much your teenage daughter knows, then decide on what examples you can use to help them understand puberty more. Just because they are young, it doesn't mean they are unaware of their own bodies.

In Closing

Parents are always trying to avoid speaking to their teenage daughters about puberty, mainly because it can be so uncomfortable for both of them to have a discussion about how the body changes. On the other hand, this conversation has to occur, so that teenage girls have the proper guidance and support throughout their journey. There are so many girls out there who don't understand what is happening to their body, and they make wrong decisions regarding their health because they lack guidance from their parents and family members. The best thing you can do, as a parent, is to help your daughter feel comfortable in her own skin. Be there to listen when she has questions, and always try your best to answer without being judgmental or embarrassed. This is a sensitive time in your daughter's life, so approach every conversation with patience and understanding.

Chapter 2:

Sex, and Other Kinds of Physical Intimacy

Talking to Your Teenage Daughter About Sex

I think most parents would agree that talking to your teenagers about sex is one of the most insanely uncomfortable things to do as a parent. Let's be realistic. No parent wants their teenager to be sexually active at a young age. There is just too much at stake if something goes wrong. Teenage pregnancies, sexually transmitted diseases, HIV/Aids and other infections, are incredibly high among the youngsters these days. As a parent, being open and honest about these things will help you educate your children so they don't make mistakes out of sheer curiosity.

When is The Right Time to Talk About Sex?

This is a question that plagues parents worldwide. When is the right time to talk about sex with your teenager? It may seem like there is never a right time, because having this talk with your child would mean that they are no longer your little boy or girl. Parents have a hard time accepting that their children are growing into adults. Time flies by, and before we know it, our kids are ready to pursue relationships and explore their sexuality. Parents should understand that it is equally embarrassing for teenagers to talk about sex with their parents, and they will try to avoid this topic for as long as they can. Don't take this as a sign that your teenager is well-educated on sex and doesn't need your help or advice. So many parents leave their teenagers to figure things out for themselves. This is a huge mistake because your teenager will seek information from their friends and from the internet.

The Times Have Changed

Because each child develops at their own pace, it's hard to decide when to have the talk with them. Some kids, as young as nine or 10, become curious about sex, whilst other kids who are older show little to no interest in sex. So how do you know whether your child is ready to talk about sex? It has a lot to do with how much your child is exposed to. There are several things that can spike your teenager's interest in sex, such as movies, friends, social media, and magazines. Back in the day, when there were no smartphones or social media around, parents would wait to talk to their kids about sex, until they were at an age where they could understand. An appropriate age would be around 16-years old, and even then parents wouldn't be too open about it with their teenagers.

During the 70s and 80s, sex was a taboo that would not be spoken of freely. Most parents would avoid the conversation altogether, leaving their teenagers to figure things out for themselves. But nowadays, the taboo has been broken. With the advancement in technology, sex is now a widespread topic that is displayed in social media and movies. No one feels uncomfortable sharing details about their sex life online, and this information is easily accessible to teenagers worldwide. They now know more about sex than most adults, thanks to the advice of their friends and technology. Parents have to be more forthcoming and open with their teenagers today. Keeping them in the dark about sex will not protect them from it. Whether you approve of it, your teenage daughter is interested in sex, and she will explore her sexuality with or without your guidance.

The Stubborn Father

Accepting that your teenage daughter is interested in sex can be a tough pill to swallow for a lot of dads out there. Fathers have a more protective side to their love, and this holds them back from accepting the fact that their daughters are growing into young women. Having the talk with your daughter can be agonizing and uncomfortable, but you have to accept that your daughter is no longer your little girl. She needs your guidance and support, and this is how you become her protector. By educating her on sex, you are equipping her with knowledge she can use to keep herself safe. Realistically speaking, you will not be there when she is exploring her sexuality, so there is no way you can protect her from making mistakes. The only way you can make sure that your daughter is being responsible is by helping her understand the purpose behind sex and the dangers that come with it.

Instinctively, girls run to their moms whenever they have "boy" issues. They feel more comfortable talking to their moms because females understand each other better. Dads come across as being stubborn and strict when talking about dating and boys. It's because of their protective side—it prevents them from being more understanding and open. Men view sex differently than women. They see it as more of a physical act, and women see it as more of an emotional act. That's why girls choose to have these conversations with their moms about sex and not their dads. Boys would feel more comfortable talking to their fathers about sex, rather than their mothers. This is a preference parents need to respect and allow.

Understanding the Signs

There are signs that parents need to be aware of that show their teenage daughter is curious about sex. Below, we explore the different signs that indicate it's the right time to talk about sex with your teenage daughter. Keep in mind that not all teenagers will display signs. Some might be more reserved than others, but it doesn't mean that they aren't interested in sex. It all depends on the personality and demeanor of your child, and as a parent, you would notice a difference in behavior which will often point to curiosity.

Asking Questions

One of the first signs that your teenager is curious about sex is when they ask questions. These questions circle around topics of sexual behavior they might have seen or heard from others. Common questions include:

- How do you kiss someone?
- Does it hurt when people have sex?
- Safe sex means what?
- How do you put on a condom?
- What is oral sex?
- What is birth control?

These are some examples of what questions teenagers will ask about sex. Parents will react shocked at first, but it's important to remain calm and think about your answer. Don't give any answers without being completely calm. You could scare away your teenagers for good. When they come to you with questions about sex, it's because they trust you, and they expect you to be honest with them.

Menstruation Starts

When your daughter gets her period, it serves as a sign that they are ready to be educated about sex. Parents should be aware of this sign, and they should start working on ways they can talk to their daughter about sex. This talk would fit into the discussion about menstruation, since a girl needs to understand why she gets her period every month. Some questions that teenage girls would ask about their period include:

- Why do I get my period?
- What is meant by ovulating?
- Why do I bleed for seven days?
- How does a girl fall pregnant?

It's imperative that your daughter have a good understanding of her period. Most girls don't have a clue what a period is, and that's how they fall pregnant at a young age. Educating your child is the best defense against teenage pregnancy, so don't leave your daughter in the dark. Have the talk with her and make her wise about her body so she can make better decisions when the time comes for her to be sexually active. Educate her on the purpose of birth control. It's one of the important aspects of sex that parents rarely talk about. If teenage girls were educated on the effectiveness of birth control from a young age, it would have drastically lowered their chances of falling pregnant.

Experimenting With Other teenagers

This is a common sign that shows your teenager is interested in sex. Try to remember your younger days. I'm sure you must have tried to experiment with other kids because you were curious about sex. At the time, you didn't have a clue what you were doing, and when your parents caught you in the act, it must have made you feel embarrassed. Your daughter is experiencing the same curiosity you once had. Be more understanding towards her. If you walk in on her experimenting with a boy, or a girl for that matter, try not to yell or be dismissive. Your reaction could have a lifelong impact on your daughter's sex life. Most parents would respond harshly if they had walked in on their teenagers experimenting with sex. This reaction would make your teenager feel that sex is bad. The right approach would be to apologize for walking in on them and then give them some space to stop their actions and work through their embarrassment. Then simply ask your daughter to have a conversation with you in private. Don't say anything embarrassing, which would make your daughter look stupid in front of the other person.

Finding Pornographic Material

Pornography has become increasingly popular nowadays, especially among teenagers. Both girls and boys display an interest in magazines, videos, and pictures that are sexual in nature. The driving force behind their interest is sheer curiosity. Teenagers want to know what sex is about, and how their body plays a role in all of this. They usually feel more comfortable exploring these things for themselves, rather than talking to their parents about it. As a parent, if you have found any type of pornographic material in your teenager's bedroom, backpack or phone, by mistake, then this could very well be a sign that it's time to have the talk with your child.

The Actual Conversation

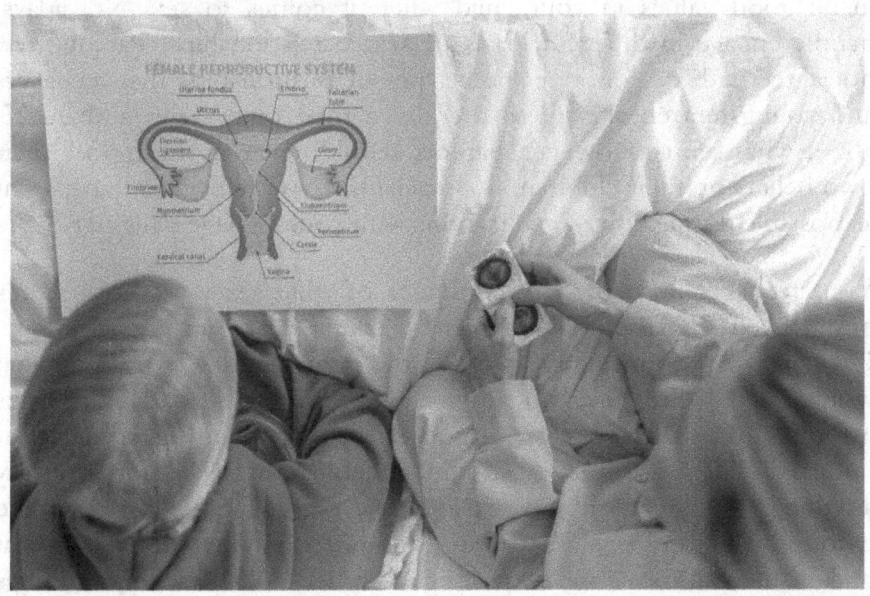

Now that you have chosen the right time to have the talk with your teenager, the next step would be to initiate the conversation. There are a lot of aspects to cover in one conversation, so it would be best if you planned out your conversation points that are most important to talk about with your teenage daughter. Sex is both good and bad, so parents need to address both sides of this coin. Don't talk about the bad only and paint a bad image of sex in your daughter's mind. This could affect her future relationships and cause her to view sex as something negative. Ensure that your conversations have a balance, so that your daughter has the chance to make up her own mind about things. Here are some important points that you should discuss with your teenage daughter about sex.

Point 1: What is Sex? And Why Do People Engage in Sex?

Sex can mean different things to different people. However, the most basic reason behind it is so human beings can express their love for their partners and procreate. It's a physical act that brings two people, who really love and care about each other, together as one. Despite the modernization of sex, and what it has become, it's important that you instill good values in your child when it comes to sex. Nowadays, people engage in different kinds of sexual relationships. Parents may not agree with or condone these types of relationships that teenagers and youngsters engage in, as they have their own views and beliefs about what sex is. However, parents should never try to impose their own beliefs on their children. It's crucial that you remain as transparent as possible during your conversations with your teenage daughter.

Your teenager probably has some idea of what sex is by now, so it's best to start off the conversation by asking her what her views are. Give her the opportunity to be forthcoming, and do nothing that would make her feel uncomfortable whilst she is sharing this information with you. It's important that you gain a clear understanding of how your daughter feels about sex before you say anything. First, you should explain how a teenager's hormones and emotions are very unstable during this phase in their lives. It's what makes them curious about exploring with their bodies and doing things that are sexual. Remember, sex isn't only about intercourse. There are other forms of sexual acts that are also popular these days, so don't leave out any information.

There are several forms of sexual activity, such as sexting, sending nude pictures, oral sex, foreplay, and sexual intercourse. Your teenager has to be properly educated in these different forms of sexual activity. This information will help them make better choices, and it won't allow them to be negatively influenced by friends or boys. I understand that it's easier said than done, but you have to be forthcoming with your teenage daughter. Some parents would say that this is TMI (too much information), but our children are being exposed to far worse things on TV and the internet. It's best that parents take charge and equip their children with knowledge from the right sources.

Point 2: Is Your Daughter Sexually Active?

This is probably one of the hardest questions to ask your teenage daughter. For boys, it isn't so difficult to find out if they have been sexually active because they won't be shy to deny it. However, with girls, it's an entirely different story. Girls are naturally shy, and they wouldn't easily reveal if they have been engaging in sexual intercourse, or in any other forms of sexual activity, especially not to their parents. So, when you are asking your daughter about whether she has been sexually active, you have to do so in a nonjudgmental way. Girls open up more towards their mothers, so it is more likely that they would be honest with their mothers or other female figures in their lives. Most parents wouldn't want to know whether their daughters are sexually active because they feel like they wouldn't be able to handle the truth. But on the other hand, it is very important that they are aware of this, so they can make sure that their children are being safe and responsible during sex. Let's face it, our kids are going to lie and go behind our backs, especially when we restrict them from doing something. So it's better if we educate them and show them there are things they can do to protect themselves from diseases and other forms of sexually transmitted illnesses. Before you pry and ask your teenage daughter about her sex life, you have to gain her trust and show her you will not be upset or angry if she is honest with you. Fear of the outcome is what will make your teenager lie and be dishonest about her sexual encounters or experiences.

Point 3: Being Safe With Sex

This is the most important aspect of sex that should be addressed during your conversation with your teenager. Parents should place a lot of importance on practicing safe sex. This is vital and should never be left out of a conversation. I think we all know how impulsive teenagers are. They rarely stop to think about the consequences of their actions before they make decisions. Whilst this spontaneity can be a good thing in other aspects of life, it isn't a good thing with being sexually active. I'm sure you remember what it's like being a teenager. You were young and carefree, doing as you pleased without giving a second thought to anything. Your daughter is in the same phase of her life now. She is ready to jump into decisions without thinking about the consequences. No matter what you say or do, she is going to do as she pleases, because that is what a teenager does. Being rebellious is a part of growing up. As a parent, you can teach your daughter about what happens when you have unprotected sex. Educate her on contraceptives and help her understand how they work. This knowledge can save her life one day, so don't hesitate to share sensitive information with your teenager. In the next section, we have broken down the topics of safe sex, teenage pregnancy and abortion. This information will help you plan out a well-structured conversation to have with your teenager.

Why Sex at a Young Age isn't a Good Idea

I think many parents will agree with the statement, "Sex at a young age is a bad idea." One of the main reasons parents don't agree with their teenagers engaging in sex is because they are not mature enough to understand what sex actually is. Teenagers, these days, have their own opinions on what sex means to them. They are easily influenced by what they see on TV, and by what they hear from friends and peers. Most teenagers believe that having sex makes you look cool, and helps you gain popularity and acceptance from other teenagers. Some girls are influenced by boys who claim having sex proves how much they love each other. There are so many reasons teenagers engage in sexual activity, and most of the time it doesn't feel right because it's being done for the wrong reasons.

When teenagers act on their instinct, without being aware of the dangers surrounding sex, it puts them at risk of falling prey to these different types of dangers. Parents have to educate their daughters on the risks that come with being sexually active at a young age. I know it can be scary talking to your teenage daughters about these things. But it's the only way you can protect them from making hasty decisions. Below, we explore the consequences that come with unprotected sex at a young age—use this information to help you educate your daughters.

Sexually Transmitted Infections

This is an important topic that should be discussed with teenage girls. Apart from HIV/Aids, there are several types of sexually transmitted infections that can ruin the lives of young girls. According to the World Health Organization, there are over 30 different viruses and parasites that are transmitted sexually. From these, only four of them are curable (*Sexually Transmitted Infections (STIs)*, n.d.). Here's a list of these infections. We explore them in more detail below.

Chlamydia

Chlamydia is one of the most common types of sexually transmitted infections, that affect women more than men. Young women are especially at risk for developing chlamydia. In 2016, there were 127 million cases of chlamydia in both men and women ages 15-49-years-old (*Sexually Transmitted Infections (STIs)*, n.d.). Chlamydia can affect several parts of the body, such as the eyes, the urinary tract, and the genital area. If left untreated, it can cause infertility in women. It could cause pelvic inflammatory disease, and it could cause blindness. This is a serious infection that could go overlooked, mainly because it has no symptoms most of the time. The only known symptom is painful urination. Chlamydia can be treated with antibiotics and other forms of herbal treatments. However, once you have been exposed to it, repeat infections are common.

Trichomoniasis

Trichomoniasis, also knows as "trich", is one of the most common types of sexually transmitted infections that can be cured. Trich is a type of parasite that lives in the lower parts of the genital tract. It is spread through unprotected sex, and even if you are using protection, chances are you can still contract it. Some signs of trich include itching, burning, painful urination, a change in the color of discharge and a foul smell. A medical professional will diagnose trich by sending a swab sample to the lab for testing. These types of infection can increase your chances of contracting HIV, and it could cause birth defects in babies, who were born to mothers who had trich while they were pregnant. In 2016, 159 million people, aged between 15-49-years-old, had tested positive for trichomoniasis. That is an astounding number of people. We can cure Trich with antibiotics, however, prevention is better than curing.

Syphilis

We can spread syphilis through sexual intercourse, as well as through oral and anal sex. Once contracted, it can leave painful sores on your genital area. There are three stages of syphilis. The first stage starts off with the spread of the sores. During the second stage, a rash appears, and in the third stage, lymph nodes become swollen. It is during the third stage, where syphilis can affect your brain and other vital organs. Many people don't even realize that they have syphilis because these symptoms go unnoticed, or brushed off as some petty rash. If left untreated, syphilis could lead to blindness, permanent brain damage, and even paralysis. It is one of the main reasons why there are so many stillbirths these days. It can be cured through an antibiotic called penicillin.

Gonorrhea

This sexually transmitted disease is known as a sex super bug because it is becoming increasingly difficult to treat. Gonorrhea is caused by bacteria which has become resistant to antibiotics. The symptoms of this infection include an urgency to urinate more often, burning and itching of the genital area. Discharge that looks like pus, or is greenish, yellowish or grayish, with a foul smell. This is a sexually transmitted infection that can cause infertility in women, and soon there might not be a cure for multi-drug resistant gonorrhea. It is mostly spread through unprotected sex, and it can develop quickly after contraction. It can be managed with medications, and in most cases, it can be cured with antibiotics.

Teenage Pregnancy

Teenage pregnancy occurs in adolescent girls between the ages of 12 and 19. Teenage girls are at risk of falling pregnant when they have unprotected sex during ovulation. Pregnancy symptoms can be the same for teenage girls, as they are for adult women, however, there is a concern for girls who are below the age of 15. Their body is still in the early stages of development, so carrying a baby could be dangerous for them. Although pregnancy in teenagers is fairly common in areas of low income and poverty-stricken communities, it doesn't mean that it will never happen to those who come from wealthy communities. Most of the low-income areas don't have access to free contraceptives, and young girls aren't educated on teenage pregnancy. Parents have the responsibility of educating their daughters and ensuring that they are aware of the consequences that come with unprotected sex.

There are a lot of parents out there today who have had their children at a young age. If you are a parent who had a child when you were a teenager, then you would understand how difficult that must have been for you. The last thing you would want is for your child to make the same choices you did when you were young. The best way you can prevent that from happening is by educating your daughter and making her aware of the various forms of contraceptives that are available today, although abstinence is the best solution. Teenagers will do as they please. No matter how much you try to educate them, ultimately, the choice is theirs. As a parent, I can understand how terrifying that must be. Letting your child make their own decisions, even after you have done your best to teach them better, is hard for parents to accept.

I remember how one of my friends helped her teenage daughter to understand the gravity of falling pregnant as a teenager. She arranged to visit one of their family members who had fallen pregnant at 16-years-old. When they visited, they could see how hard life was for the family member. She had to drop out of school, stay home and take care of the baby, who was now 4-months-old, and she had to find a way to support her child. Life wasn't easy, yes the baby brought an immense amount of happiness, but she just wasn't ready to be a mother yet. The sleepless nights, the constant crying, it was all too much to handle. My friend's daughter really opened her eyes after that visit. It helped her see things from a different perspective. Oftentimes, teenagers turn a deaf ear whenever their parents try to have an important conversation with them. So, in order to get the message across, you have to help them catch a glimpse of reality. When you are addressing this topic with your teenager, consider showing them a video of a teenage mother's experience. This will help them get a deeper understanding of how serious this conversation is.

Different Forms of Contraceptives

- condoms (male and female)
- contraceptive pills
- morning-after pills
- contraceptive injections
- IUD

The above are examples of the different contraceptives available today. However, the hormones in these contraceptives aren't healthy for an adolescent girl. Your daughter's body is still developing and taking contraceptives for a long period could cause fertility issues in the future. The best way to stay safe is to abstain from sexual intercourse. However, if they are going to be sexually active, then a condom is the safest option. I know this could be extremely uncomfortable for you to talk about with your daughter, but the increased numbers in sexually transmitted infections and teenage pregnancies, calls for these important conversations to be had with your teenagers.

In Closing

Think back to the time when your parents sat you down and gave you "the talk". How did that make you feel? At what age did you have your first sexual encounter? Do you have any regrets? These are a few important questions you could ask yourself before you talk to your teenage daughter. Putting yourself in her shoes will be incredibly helpful in working out what to say and how to say it. There are so many important aspects of sex to address with your child, and because this topic is so sensitive, you cannot spend too much time talking about it with your teenager. They will become fidgety, and you will lose their attention. So summarize the most important key points, and lay them down during the conversion. You don't have to go into much detail, as it could make your daughter feel uncomfortable. Try to keep your tone friendly and nonjudgmental. This will help your teenager be more accepting of the information you will share with her. Speak to other parents and ask them what works and what doesn't when it comes to speaking to their children about sex. Remember to take down notes so you don't forget. Sharing experiences will help you get a glimpse of how other parents are carrying out their conversations, so you could use some pointers from them as well.

Chapter 3:

Peer Pressure and its Consequences

How Peer Pressure Affects a Teenage Girl's Life

What Is Peer Pressure?

Peer pressure occurs when a group of teenagers, or one teenager, coerces or influences another individual to engage in certain activities or behavior that they are not comfortable with. The truth is, 85% of high school kids have admitted that they have felt pressure from their friends to engage in certain activities that they wouldn't otherwise engage in. Almost 75% of teenagers have experimented with alcohol because of peer pressure, and 65% of teenage girls felt pressured to lose their virginity (September 10 & Pediatrics, 2013). Peer pressure often gets overlooked by teenagers who are desperate to fit in. Even though peer pressure is being addressed by teachers and parents, teenagers still fall into the trap. It's awfully difficult to build true friendships these days, so your teenager might have a tough time finding a group of friends they are comfortable with. When they do find friends, there are certain things they have to do in order to fit in. Your teenager might not be comfortable doing these things, but they do it anyway, just so they can find their place and be liked by their new group of peers. Whether it's about changing their appearance or picking up a bad habit, your teenage daughter is unknowingly being pressured to fit in.

Joining a group of friends that engages in smoking cigarettes and drinking alcohol is much more common these days. Even if your daughter has never smoked a cigarette before, she would feel pressured to start now because she wants to be a part of the group. Every teenager wants to be cool and well-known by others. They are willing to go to any extent to fit in and not look like a loser. There are different forms of peer pressure. Most people aren't aware they are being influenced, or that they are influencing others. Teenagers who want to dominate others often use peer pressure to get what they want. They don't understand how it affects the other person, or how much damage their behavior causes. It's important that you help your child understand the different types of peer pressure, so they can identify situations where peer pressure comes up. Let's take a look at the different forms of peer pressure used by people today.

Types of Peer Pressure

Peer pressure involves communicating a message across for the other person to pick up on. Communication can involve spoken messages, unspoken messages, indirect peer pressure, and direct peer pressure. We explore these in more detail below.

Spoken Peer Pressure

This type of peer pressure is communicated verbally. It occurs when one individual, or a group of people, asks another individual to do something they are not comfortable with. It is a powerful form of peer pressure, as it involves clear words or instructions on what to do and how to do it. When you actually hear a spoken instruction, it's hard to ignore the message.

Unspoken Peer Pressure

Unspoken peer pressure occurs in situations where an individual is present while others are engaging in risky behavior and doing things they are not supposed to be doing. The individual who is watching feels a certain type of pressure to behave in the same way in order to fit in and be a part of the group. This type of peer pressure is quite common, and even though words aren't spoken, the message is very clear about what needs to be done.

Direct Peer Pressure

This can be spoken or unspoken, and often involves influencing someone to do something on the spot. When an individual is placed in an uncomfortable situation, where they are required to do something immediately, it can be very stressful for them. It's a "now or never" type of situation, where the individual does not have time to think about their actions or the consequences.

Indirect Peer Pressure

This type of peer pressure can be unspoken, spoken, direct or indirect, and it speaks to our own curiosity about wanting to try certain things. When your daughter sees someone else doing something, she will suddenly wonder what it would be like to engage in this type of behavior. Indirect peer pressure also sparks her interests and validates her desire to try these things.

The Difference between Positive and Negative Influence From Peers

Peer pressure isn't always a bad thing. Just as there are two sides to a coin, there are also two sides to peer pressure. There can be positive peer pressure and negative peer pressure. Positive peer pressure involves influencing someone to do something that is good for them and for the surrounding people. A good example would be your daughter signing up for the all-girls' soccer club, because she has joined a new group of friends who all play soccer, and she wants to be a part of that. There are teenagers out there who have the power to influence others positively. These types of friends are good for your teenage daughter, as they will influence her to try new things and find out what her true talents are. They will inspire her to be better every day, and she will have a desire to achieve.

The negative side of peer pressure, as mentioned in the previous sections, involves influencing others to be a part of unhealthy, dangerous, and risky behavior. Smoking, drinking alcohol, drugs, and sex are the most common behaviors that are involved in negative peer pressure. This kind of peer pressure could ruin the lives of your teenagers. Substance abuse is dangerous, and most teenagers don't realize that they are doing something wrong because they are told that these things make you look cool. Your teenage daughter might see her friends smoking marijuana, and she would want to try it, even though she knows it's wrong. Watching her friends skip classes or having multiple sexual partners would give her the wrong message. She will think it's okay to take part in these types of things just because her friends are doing it. It's up to the parents to educate their children on the difference in peer pressure.

You cannot expect your child to know this because they are experiencing these things for the first time. Your daughter will make mistakes, and her judgment will be poor because she has zero experience with the outside world. Our kids rely on us, their parents, to guide them and teach them about the world. Even though your daughter might not seem interested in what you have to say, it is still imperative that you talk to her and teach her about the difference in positive and negative peer pressure.

Being Pressured by Parents and Family Members

To be honest, parents also pressure their children into doing things they aren't comfortable with. There are millions of teenagers out there who will agree with me when I say that parents expect their children to live up to their dreams. As parents, we all have dreams for our children. The day we bring them into this world, we start planning their future. In the back of our minds, we already know what careers we want them to have, we plan out their weddings years in advance, and we know what hobbies they will be interested in. Seems like a pretty solid plan except for the fact that we don't stop to think about what our kids would want. It's because of these dreams and plans we create for our children that we pressure them into living a certain way. Parents influence their kids to do a number of things. Even though you have your child's best interest at heart, you could be hurting them by crushing their own dreams to make yours a reality.

Most parents don't even realize they have been pressuring their children or influencing them. Training your child, from a young age, to be interested in a particular sport or field of education, is a normal thing parents do. But when they reach an age where they are mature enough to decide what they want, parents should back off and allow their children to make the right decisions for themselves. Don't force them or bribe them into doing something they don't want to do. It can affect their self-confidence and cause issues with their mental health.

Try your best to guide them in the right direction, and offer them advice on what careers and hobbies they should pursue, but never make it seem like they don't have an option. They should be able to make their own decisions without being swayed or issued with an ultimatum.

Strategies You Could Share with Your Child to Cope With Peer Pressure

Dealing with peer pressure can be incredibly frustrating and nerve-wrecking for a teenage girl. There is more pressure placed on females to fit in because girls have higher standards of perfection. When it comes to sex, drugs, and alcohol, females are more hesitant to engage in these activities than males are. It's difficult to influence a girl, or to pressure her into doing something, because she will play it over and over in her mind before she agrees. Engaging in behaviors and activities that she is not comfortable with can cause feelings of guilt, frustration and shame. This is a huge burden for such a small person to bear alone. There are things that parents can do to help their teen daughters cope with peer pressure. Below, we take a look at a few tips you can share with your child to help her overcome peer pressure.

Be Confident Enough to Walk Away

Teenagers who give in to peer pressure usually lack the confidence in themselves to say no. They believe there is something lacking in themselves, and the only way they will be accepted is if they do whatever their friends and peers are doing. Automatically, this will make them "good enough" to be a part of the group. Parents have to encourage their children to find their lost confidence so they can stand up for themselves and not give in to peer pressure. It can be difficult to turn down friends and say no to taking part in various activities or behaviors. But when your teenager is confident in themselves, they won't have a problem in saying no and standing their ground. This is important, not only for their wellbeing during adolescence, but also for the rest of their lives. This is the stage in life where your daughter must learn how to assert herself. If she gives in to peer pressure because of her low self-confidence, then this behavior could become a pattern that follows her into adult life.

Choose Positive Peers

Parents must help their children choose friends that have a more positive and friendly attitude. Teenagers have difficulty choosing friends who are a positive influence on them because everyone is drawn to the cool kids. Help your teenage daughter understand that just because these kids look cool, it doesn't mean they are a positive influence. Your daughter should be able to identify positivity in others. Here are a few ways you can explain to your child what positive people look like.

Positive Friends Are

- Focused on school and are dedicated to their studies.
- Ambitious. They have goals and dreams.
- Respectful when they speak to others, and about others.
- Confident in themselves enough to say no to peer pressure.
- Welcoming towards new people, and they don't ask you to do anything to be a part of their group.
- Helpful and supportive in times of need.
- Peacekeepers. They always try to avoid conflict and work through issues calmly.

Negative Friends Are

- Selfish, they always think about their own needs and wants.
- Cruel and mean. They don't care about your feelings. As long as they get what they want, they will be nice towards you.

- Controlling. They want to tell you what to do, when to do it, and how to do it.
- Unsupportive and they are never around to help you when you need them.
- Pressurize you into doing things you don't want to do.
- Talk about you behind your back, and make fun of you.
- They don't have goals or dreams that they want to pursue in life.
- They thrive in chaos, and they love to cause problems.

Create Boundaries and Enforce Them

As parents, we like to set safe limits for our children to follow, and we encourage them not to step over the line. While this is all well and good, it's also important to explain to your children why you have set these limits for them. This will help them understand the importance behind every rule you set, and what would happen if they didn't follow them. In the long run, this process will teach your child that it is important for them to have their own boundaries and limits set when it comes to interacting with others. The first thing you should do is explain what boundaries are and how they help protect you. Everyone has boundaries, and I'm sure you must have heard people say, "don't overstep my boundaries" or "stay within your limits". People set boundaries as a way of communicating that they have certain lines that cannot be crossed. For instance, if your teenage daughter tells her friends she doesn't like people smoking around her because she has asthma and her friends disregard what she asked of them and smoke anyway, then they are overstepping her boundaries.

Parents must help their daughters identify their boundaries and teach them how to reinforce them out there in the world. It is crucial that your daughter has limits and boundaries to keep herself from being easily swayed by others. It will help her stand her ground by giving her something to believe in. Once she has identified her boundaries, she has to learn how to reinforce them around others. This means being clear and precise about what she will and will not tolerate, as far as making friends and participating in certain activities. Reinforcing boundaries helps people see your daughter means business when it comes to certain things about her life. And when she sets limits, it helps people know where they stand with her and how far they can go before overstepping her limits. Remember, people don't know these things unless you make it known to them. Educate your daughter and make sure that she is always verbal about her feelings when people are overstepping her boundaries.

Always Talk About Their Feelings

If your teenage daughter has encountered peer pressure at any point in her life, she should open up and talk about her experience. Peer pressure can have a traumatic effect on teenagers, and when they keep these feelings bottled up, it can lead to depression and even suicide. Encourage your child to open up about her feelings. Assure her you will do your best to help her, no matter what has transpired. If your teenager is hesitant, be patient and show her you will always be here when she is ready to share. Sometimes all your child needs is to know that they have your love and support. This can make a huge difference. If you need to seek professional help for your child, don't hesitate to do so. Speaking to a therapist or counselor might help lessen their fears, guilt, and shame that has developed because of peer pressure.

If others have bullied and abused your child, you have to take action immediately. In most cases, bullies use peer pressure to get what they want from other kids. If these kids don't deliver, these bullies then beat and embarrass them. This can have a lifelong impact on your teenager. So if this is the case with your child, make sure you are getting all the help you can to make sure that your child is removed from that situation immediately. Change schools if you have to, get your child checked out by a doctor, and be there to support your child through their recovery.

In Closing

Peer pressure can be avoided. It is not a long-term issue that cannot be solved. Parents can teach their children how to stand up for themselves and say no to bullies. Your daughter has to build a strong confidence in herself that will carry her through any situation she faces in life. It all starts at home. When parents empower their children and allow them to have a voice, they are also training them to stand up against the things they don't believe in. When parents teach their children how to set boundaries, they are also helping them to protect themselves. The key to overcoming peer pressure is to stay clear from people who are not positive influences, and to stand your ground when someone tries to influence you negatively. Make it a priority to build up your daughter's self-confidence and teach her how to identify negative people that may try to lure her in and take advantage of her.

Chapter 4:
Teenage Depression

Depression and Anxiety in Adolescence

Depression is a dark pit that swallows a person without warning. It does not choose its victims, and oftentimes people don't even realize they are depressed. Natasha was in a similar situation. Natasha was a 13-year-old teenage girl who had been feeling very down and out since she started high school. She used to be a bubbly kid, who enjoyed playing soccer, and she loved participating in different sports. A few months after starting high school, Natasha began to experience mood swings, and she noticed she was always angry about something or the other. She didn't understand why she was feeling this way. Natasha stopped playing soccer because she lost interest in the sport. She didn't enjoy hanging out with friends as much as she used to before, and she was always feeling empty and sad.

At the time, Natasha didn't understand what was going on with her. She felt very emotional all the time, and she became increasingly depressed. No one could understand why Natasha was feeling this way. And her parents didn't notice there was something going on with their daughter because they were always working. Natasha began experiencing episodes of depression that became severe over time, and this affected her ability to live a normal teenage life. The only time her parents took notice was when Natasha tried to take her own life. When she was hospitalized, a psychologist spoke to her parents and told them that Natasha was suicidal because she was clinically depressed. Her depression wasn't because of any problems she had been experiencing. It was because of a chemical imbalance in her brain.

She needed to be put on medication to help her control her depression. Once her depression eased, there was no reason for her to take her life again. This all could have been avoided if only her parents paid attention to the signs. Parents can sometimes miss signs of depression in their teenagers because they don't pay enough attention to the signs. The mistake so many parents make is they think teenagers don't suffer from depression. These parents are under the impression that their teenagers are young, carefree, and living life, so how could they possibly be depressed? When the signs are ignored, or missed out on, the situation gets worse, and teenagers spiral out of control. Some of them become involved with drugs and alcohol, and some become so severely depressed that they commit suicide. In this chapter, we aim to help parents understand why their teenage daughters are prone to depression, and we also include great tips to help parents identify the signs of depression.

Why is Depression Common Among Teenagers?

Teenagers lead pretty difficult lives, believe it or not. Most people wouldn't agree with that statement because they only see as far as the surface. Nobody looks deep enough to see the struggles that teenagers have to face daily. Not even their own parents understand the amount of stress they have to deal with. You might be wondering what kinds of stress are teenagers facing in their lives? Well, there are a lot of things that stress teenagers out. We will look at different aspects of life that cause stress in your teenager's life.

The Pressures of School

School can be an extremely frustrating and stressful place for a teenager. A survey was carried out by the American Physiological Association to find out how many teenagers are stressed out about school. They found that 45% of teenagers admitted that school stressed them out a lot (Neighmond, 2013). The large volume of assignments and projects isn't something exciting to look forward to. Teenagers spend hours in lessons, trying to pay attention and focusing on what is being taught. Most of the time, they don't understand what is going on in these classrooms, which causes a great deal of frustration. Meeting deadlines on assignments, and making sure that all the criteria are met, can be very stressful. Teenagers won't share their frustrations with their family because they don't want to be judged by them. Instead, they will hide their emotions and make it seem as if everything is normal. So don't beat yourself up if you haven't noticed how stressed your teenager is because of school.

Almost 80% of the time, parents realize their child is struggling in school when they see the report card, or when the teacher calls them in to discuss the child's progress. The pressures of excelling and getting good grades become too much for most teenagers to bear. Girls tend to be more competitive than boys, so they have a harder time accepting that their grades are poor. Parents also add on to the stress when they pressure their children to achieve a certain grade in each subject. A+, B+, nothing less than perfect grades are expected by controlling parents who don't understand how much work goes into achieving those high grades. When your child feels as if she is not good enough at her studies, it will cause her self-esteem to drop considerably. If there is a learning disability involved, it will be harder to achieve top marks in academics, which may lead to further embarrassment and depression among teenagers.

Family Conflict

Family conflict is one of the major reasons teenagers suffer from depression at such a young age. Home is where your child spends most of their time, so it's safe to say that this should be a happy place for them. After you've had a long, tiring day at work, you look forward to coming home and taking refuge in the arms of your family. Your daughter feels the same way. After a hard day at school, or after a fun time with friends, she looks forward to coming home and spending time with her family. But what happens when she comes home to a toxic environment? Parents arguing non-stop with each other, dad is an alcoholic or mom is always fighting about money, siblings involved in drugs and violence, sexual abuse from a family member, or parents fighting with their own children. These are some common types of issues that go on in the homes of millions of families.

Families have their disagreements once in a while. But when these fights become a daily occurrence, it can cause severe psychological damage to the children that are living in the home. This emotional trauma can follow them right up into their adolescent years, especially if the bickering and fighting has continued throughout the years. Parents wouldn't even notice that their children are falling into depression because they are always busy arguing with everyone. They take out their frustrations on their kids, and they don't stop to think about how it's going to affect their children in the long run. When a child is exposed to violence from a young age, it traumatizes them severely. They will eventually get used to seeing it every day in their homes, but this doesn't mean it doesn't affect them anymore. They carry the emotional burden on them, and it manifests into depression and anxiety.

Peer Pressure

As mentioned in the previous section, peer pressure can have a huge negative impact on a person's emotional wellbeing and state of mind. If your teenager has been a victim of peer pressure, there is a high possibility that there is some type of emotional distress or anxiety that has developed over time. With so many emotions all felt at the same time, it can be challenging to self-regulate the negative feelings. Fear, anxiety, shame, and guilt are examples of the type of feelings an individual will encounter when they are pressured to do something they aren't comfortable doing. Since peer pressure is a form of bullying, it can leave a deep dent in the self-confidence of your teenage daughter. The level of manipulation that takes place is astounding. Your teenager would take all the blame for her wrong actions, without even realizing that her friends and peers had manipulated her.

Keeping so much guilt and shame inside isn't healthy for anyone, let alone a teenager. Sometimes, the consequences of their actions result in serious incidents where people's lives could be destroyed forever. When this happens, it adds to the guilt and shock that an individual experiences. These are the types of situations parents try so hard to avoid. However, teenagers will be teenagers, and they often make mistakes which they must learn from. Put yourself in your child's shoes for a few minutes. Don't think like a parent. Just imagine that you are a teenager who has been pressured by your friends to smoke marijuana every morning before class. You know that it's not a good idea because you won't be able to concentrate on the lesson, but you do it anyway because you don't want your friends to think you're bored. Every day you do the same thing and feel terrible afterwards. Can you imagine how frustrating life can become? Depression will most definitely sneak its way into your life. It can be difficult to see the signs of depression in your teenager, especially when they like to lock themselves up in their rooms and avoid all contact with family.

Young Love

Yes, you read that right. Falling in love, at a ripe age, is one of the most exciting phases of a teenage girl's life. Although they're too young to understand what love really is, to them, crushing on the most popular boy at school might seem like true love. While harmless infatuation is normal in adolescence, it can quickly turn ugly when teenagers become too involved. Experiencing the first heartbreak is something every girl will go through in her lifetime. Being dumped by a boy you had a crush on is extremely embarrassing. This can be very painful, and it can cause a lot of emotional distress because your teenage daughter might think that she isn't good enough. Further problems with her self-esteem will arise, causing depression. Teenagers are very impressionable, so whatever experiences they go through, it will stay with them for the rest of their lives. Everyone will remember their first heartbreak because the experience will be very traumatic.

Sexual or Physical Abuse

Sexual and physical abuse are strong triggers for depression and anxiety. These are traumatic experiences that really break a person's soul up from the inside. When teenagers are sexually abused, it often gets swept under the rug by a lot of family members. Whether it happened in the past, or in recent days, the effect it has on a girl's life is devastating. Teenage girls fall prey to sexual predators who lurk within families, at school, and in public places. The majority of the time, teenage girls are sexually and physically abused by a family member or a family friend, or by someone they know personally from school, like a friend or an acquaintance. Victims of sexual abuse don't just recover overnight. It takes years to start the healing process, and they have to face triggers on a daily basis. These triggers could be looking at a scar that was made during an assault, or hearing a certain song, or smelling a certain perfume.

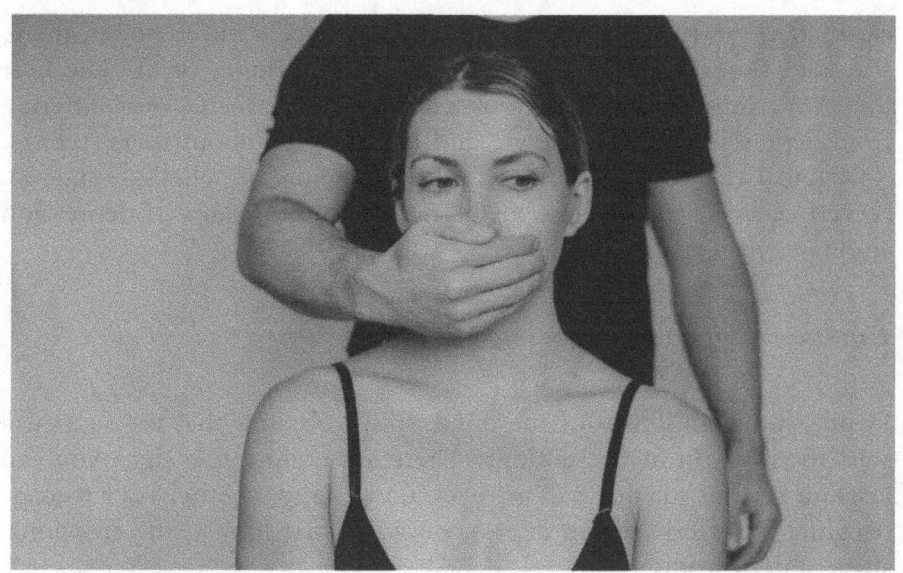

Anything that brings back traumatic memories of that assault will act as a trigger and set off a whole range of negative emotions. Sometimes this can be good for the healing process, but other times, it could cause setbacks or delays in the healing. Depression sets in quickly when it comes to sexual and physical abuse. The experience, being so traumatic and life changing, alters a person's emotional state and sends them into a downward spiral of depression and anxiety. Living life in fear or what's going to happen next, being anxious about being around people, and developing panic attacks that become a regular part of life are all forms of anxiety. Most parents wouldn't be aware of a situation like this, because it would be difficult for teenagers to open up and talk about sexual abuse. There is a vast amount of shame and guilt that is felt by the victim, even though they aren't at fault. If you suspect your teenage daughter has been a victim of sexual or physical abuse, it would be wise to seek professional help.

Signs Of Depression in Teenagers

Adolescence can be a very difficult phase for a teenager, as they are experiencing many changes, both physically and emotionally. The signs of depression among teenagers won't be difficult to catch if parents pay close attention to their children. You will notice a difference in them, and sometimes it can be challenging to put a finger on it. The best thing for parents to do, if they are not sure if their teenager is suffering from depression, is to sit down and talk to them about their feelings. This will help you get a better understanding of what's going on. Nevertheless, here are some of the most common signs of depression among teenagers.

Emotional Signs of Depression

Depression is an illness of the mind, so it's obvious that the signs will start to show through emotions. There are quite a few signs you can keep an eye out for that will help you understand whether your teenage daughter is suffering from depression. Let's first look at the emotional signs of depression.

Sadness and Hopelessness

This is one of the most common signs of depression in people. The initial feelings of sadness sets in during the early stages of depression. Your teenager might have been a very optimistic person who loved to have fun. But now, you notice she is always sad and quiet. She doesn't seem to smile as much as she used to, and she isn't looking forward to her future. She doesn't want to make plans for college, and she talks about being the same way for the rest of her life. Everything she says nowadays has an ominous tone to it. She no longer looks forward to happy occasions, such as birthdays or hanging out with friends, and she feels she is better off alone.

Anger and Attitude

Anger brings out the worst in everyone, and unfortunately, people who suffer from depression can be easily angered. Your teenager might be displaying signs of anger that have become more common lately. She snaps over the smallest of issues, and she has an attitude with friends and family members. Whenever you try to talk to her, she becomes irritated and shuts you out. Everyone seems like an enemy to her, and she is always on edge. The family walks on eggshells around her because they are afraid she will become angry and lash out without warning. This is an example of how a teenage girl can display her anger.

Rebellious Behavior

Rebellion is another common sign of depression, especially among teenagers. It starts off small, as your teenager might just ignore you when you are speaking, or she might disobey an instruction you have given her. If parents overlook it, the behavior of their teenager escalates in a short period of time. You will notice that your daughter refuses to study, or help with the household chores. Whenever you try to reprimand her behavior, she will have an attitude and rebel against you. Everything that she is not allowed to do, she does it to get a response out of you. She becomes disrespectful, starts using vulgar words, and she no longer wants to do anything as a family.

Mood Swings

Depression causes intense mood swings that can make someone lose their personality. One moment your teenager can be happy and easygoing, the next moment she is feeling sad and lost. These constant changes in emotions can be exhausting, which is why teenagers spend most of their time alone in their rooms. The solitude helps them refuel to face another hectic day. Because their brains are still developing, teenagers would find it hard to understand what is going on with their moods. So they feel the best way for them to deal with their feelings is by being alone, or by acting out or engaging in risky behavior. If you notice your teenager isn't behaving like themselves anymore, it could indicate that they are dealing with depression.

Constant Crying

Emotional outbursts are a common sign of depression. Sometimes it can be hard to keep all the negative feelings inside, and the only way to find relief from the torment of depression is to cry and let it all out. If you notice your teenager crying regularly, even for the smallest reasons, she could be suffering from depression. Depressed people have this dark cloud hovering above them all the time, and no matter how hard they try to control their emotions, it becomes too much to handle. Most of the time, teenagers try to avoid crying in front of their family, so parents could not pick up on this easily. However, there are a few signs you could keep an eye out for.

- puffiness around the eyes
- eyes are reddish
- constant headaches
- runny nose

Whilst these signs could point to a number of different things, like allergies or the common cold, changes in behavior and becoming withdrawn from the family, coupled with these other signs, could indicate that your teenager isn't suffering from a cold. Depression is long term, so the signs wouldn't automatically disappear after a few days. You will notice these signs on a constant basis, and that is how you understand your teenager is going through something.

Physical Signs of Depression

Bad Grades at School

Teenagers who suffer from depression cannot perform well at school. In fact, a drastic drop in grades is one of the first signs that shows there is something going on with your teenager. If your teenager was an intelligent student who enjoyed studying and getting top grades, a sudden drop in their performance should alarm you as a parent. You would instantly know there is something big going on that is affecting your child's ability to perform well at school. Teachers are the first to pick up on a student's performance, and when they see a constant decline, it can cause concern. Parents are usually notified by teachers to figure out what the problem is. Depression is a constant battle within the mind, which explains why your teenager cannot focus on anything else, and her performance at school is affected. Parents should not overlook this or take it lightly. As soon as you notice a change in your child's grades at school, sit down and have a conversation with your child. Try to get to the heart of the issue, so that you can help your child before things get worse.

Change in Appetite and Body Weight

People who are living with depression experience changes to their appetite. Some people eat more because they find comfort and relief from food, whilst others lose their appetite and desire for food. As a parent, you should have a good idea of your child's relationship with food. Does your daughter eat more when she is stressed? Or does she avoid eating until she is more relaxed and stress-free? Being aware of your daughter's eating habits is important because it can help you pick up on signs that could indicate there is something going on with your child. A drastic change in body weight could show that your child has been dealing with something difficult emotionally that is taking a toll on her body physically. Dealing with depression is a battle, and for most people, taking care of themselves is no longer a priority. So, they eat unhealthy foods, and they don't necessarily worry about how it's going to affect their health. Some people go as far as starving themselves just because they are stressed out or depressed about food. If your teenager isn't maintaining a healthy appetite or body weight, and if she is struggling emotionally as well, it could indicate that she is depressed and frustrated about certain issues in her life.

Cuts and Bruises on Body

When depression becomes severe, teenagers have a hard time controlling their feelings. The overwhelming emotions cannot be bottled up any longer, and the only way to find relief is to express what you are feeling on the inside. Some teenagers express their emotions by cutting themselves to find relief. Parents will notice cuts on the wrists, hands or thighs of their teenagers. Most of the time, they will try to cover up their scars. For example, on a scorching hot day, your teenager would use a jacket or long sleeve shirt to cover her arms. Or she wouldn't let you touch her, out of fear that you would see her cuts. Apart from the cutting, teenagers might also have bruises on their knuckles or around their hands, which indicates that they have been punching doors, walls, or floors. This is another way they chose to release the negative emotions that are weighing them down.

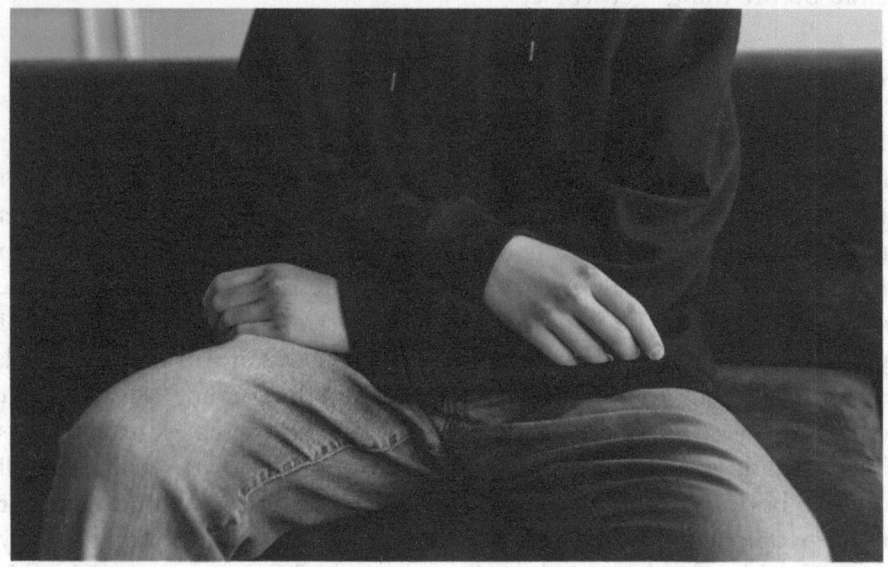

Poor Dressing and Untidiness

Depression makes you lose all interest in yourself, and that includes your interest in keeping yourself neat and well-dressed. Truth be told, when a person is depressed, they lose touch with reality because they are pushed into this dark hole where life stops. There is no sense of time, and each day blends in with the next, creating an endless loop of day and night. There is a constant battle to get through each moment, and this really affects a person's state of mind. The same would happen to your teenager if she was experiencing depression. She would lose interest in the way she dressed, and pajamas would become the only thing she would use. Her hair would be unkempt, and her overall appearance can be very untidy. In severe cases of depression, teenagers will skip showers and won't even get out of bed to brush their teeth.

Substance Abuse

Teenagers often become involved with drugs and alcohol when they are dealing with depression. Yes, teenagers will experiment with drugs and alcohol from time to time. However, when it gets out of hand, that is a problem. Parents will notice a sudden change in the behavior of their teenagers, such as staying out late frequently, coming home intoxicated most days, and having regular mood swings. This type of risky behavior can be very dangerous for teenage girls, so parents need to be more attentive and aggressive when it comes to helping their teenagers. If not addressed in a timely manner, substance abuse can spiral out of control, causing lifelong issues which affect every aspect of your teenagers' life.

How are Teenagers Diagnosed With Depression?

Diagnosing depression in teenagers can sometimes be a bit tricky. During adolescence, a teenager experiences changes in their hormones which lead to mood swings. There are so many new areas of life that become available to explore, and this can either have a negative effect or a positive effect on their state of mind. However, sometimes depression can go undetected because parents try to explain away the signs by saying it's just a phase. Depression is an illness of the mind, so there are not many tests that can be done to diagnose it. If you are unsure about your child being depressed, there are other ways to find out the truth. Below, we take a look at some ways that medical professionals used to diagnose depression.

Psychiatric Evaluation

A psychiatric evaluation is often conducted by a medical professional, such as a psychologist, who will sit down with your teenager and ask them a few questions about themselves. This evaluation is usually done privately, and parents aren't allowed inside the room. This gives your teenager the freedom and privacy to speak about whatever they want without the fear of being judged by their parents. Sometimes, just one session isn't enough to issue a diagnosis. A psychologist might require two or three sessions so they can get a bigger picture of what's going on inside your teenager's mind. In severe cases, where there is worry about suicide, an evaluation is done within a few minutes whilst your child has been admitted to the healthcare facility. All in all, the medical professional will consult family and friends to find out what changes they have noticed, and they will look at the child's grades at school.

Physical Examination

A medical practitioner, such as a doctor, will carry out a physical examination of your teenager. The doctor will look for signs of depression that manifest physically. Some examples of these signs include weight loss or gain, cuts or bruises on the body, lack of basic hygiene, and checking blood pressure to evaluate for anxiety. These tests can give a good indication if someone is experiencing depression. As mentioned in the previous section, depression can be seen just by looking at a person. It affects an individual, as most people would say, in a way that they no longer recognize someone who has been dealing with depression, because their entire appearance changes. When someone has been fighting a battle daily, it will begin to show on the outside.

What are The Warning Signs that Indicate Your Teenager is Headed for Suicide?

Depression can escalate quite fast in teenagers, especially when they don't have support from friends and family. Dealing with something so agonizing all alone can have a massive impact on the emotional and physical wellbeing of an individual. Suicide is a possibility when it comes to severe depression. Parents need to be aware of the signs that point to suicidal behavior in their teenage daughters. It can be difficult to read teenagers, and most of the time parents have no clue their child is so unhappy. And when their kids take their own lives, it comes as a complete shock to them. Here are a few signs parents should look out for in their teenagers' behavior.

Withdrawing from Family and Friends

Becoming distant from family and friends seems like a good idea for a teenager who is contemplating suicide. In their minds, they feel it's best if they move further away from the people they love, so it will be easier to take their own lives. Parents must be weary when they notice their teenager has been spending a lot of time alone, especially when they are upset or going through a rough patch. Your child would need your full support and encouragement during this time, so try to make sure that you are not judging them or making them feel uncomfortable.

Teenagers also become distant because they don't want family or friends finding out about their plans to commit suicide, so they choose to limit contact with others. Giving your teenager space whilst they are going through depression is very important. However, keep a close eye on them just to make sure that they are not falling into the wrong mindset. Too much time spent alone could result in wrong choices being made.

Talking About Suicide and Writing Suicide Notes

People who have been thinking about ending their own lives often say things like "I know you would be better if I was dead", or "Don't worry, I will be gone soon enough, so don't worry about me." Sometimes when parents hear their teenagers talking like this, they simply brush it off as their teenager being dramatic. They don't take it seriously enough until their kids have ended their lives. We can understand that teenagers will be dramatic from time to time, especially girls, but this doesn't mean you should just ignore her. You, as the parent, must do whatever you can to be sure of your daughter's mindset when she is saying these things.

Parents may also stumble across notes or letters that have disturbing messages pertaining to suicide. Notes that read, "I'm sorry for all the pain I've caused. Now that I'm gone, there won't be any more pain." You might find these notes crumbled up in the trash can, or you might find them among your daughter's belongings. If you do happen to stumble upon something like this, please don't take it lightly. Get your child the help she needs immediately, before it's too late.

Engaging in Risky Behavior

A suicidal teenager wouldn't care about their own wellbeing. Engaging in risky behavior, such as driving whist intoxicated or running out into open traffic, is a warning sign your teenager might be suicidal. This type of crazy behavior might seem daring to others, but for your teenager, it could be a cry for help. Parents must ensure they pay attention to how their teenager is behaving, especially if she isn't usually the type to take risks or live dangerously. Teenagers tend to take risks when they are suicidal because they have a hope that maybe something will happen to them whilst they are doing these risky things. It sounds terrifying; I know. A teenager would have to be in a lot of emotional turmoil if she wanted to end her life so badly. It's any parent's worst nightmare, to find out how unhappy their kids are. So much so that they are desperate to end their lives any chance they get.

As hard as this might be for you to comprehend, you have to make sure you identify these kinds of risky behavior in your teenager. If you feel like they are being too reckless and unlike their usual self, then you need to have a conversation with your child. Teenagers are reckless, but there is a categorical difference between the levels of recklessness that they engage in. Parents just have to be alert when it comes to their children.

Extreme Mood Changes

One of the main reasons people commit suicide is because they cannot handle the turmoil any longer. Whatever was holding them down has finally got the best of them, and now there isn't any reason to hold on and fight because life has become so unbearable. These intense feelings of guilt, shame, anger, and fear become so intense it takes over an individual's life. A teenager does not have the ability to self-regulate their emotions yet, as their brains are still developing. So it will be harder for them to be patient with themselves and work through their feelings. Parents will notice their teenager becoming more irritable, sad, anxious, and lost. They would slowly lose touch with reality as the days go by. Parents will notice their teenagers reacting more intensely to situations that could be handled calmly. They will have no control over their emotions—snapping at any time for any reason.

Giving Stuff Away

If you have noticed your teenager giving all of their prized possessions away to their friends or family members for no apparent reason, then this could be a cause for concern; especially if this is accompanied by other major signs of depression and suicide. When a teenager is planning to commit suicide, one of the first things they do is give away all of their stuff that means so much to them. They know they will not be around much longer, so they give away their cherished items, so their friends and family can benefit more from them. This is how you know they are being serious about ending their lives, because they are giving away things that are a part of their lives. Items might include clothing, shoes, jewelry, books, laptops, cellphones, money, and so on.

Speaking to Your Teenager About Suicide

Suicide is a sensitive topic to discuss with your teenage daughter. However, it is necessary that parents take the time to sit down with their children and discuss the importance of mental health. No parent wants to live in fear of waking up one day to find out that their teenager has taken their own lives. Whilst there is little that can be done to prevent your teenager from experiencing hard times in their lives, there are other ways to make sure your teenager is capable of handling these hard times on their own. Parents will always be there to guide their children, no matter how young they are or how old they get. But there will be instances where you cannot be around your teenager all the time, so they should be able to regulate their emotions on their own. Below, we take a look at ways that you can help your teenager through a difficult phase in their lives.

Prepare for the Conversation

Planning is essential when it comes to having sensitive conversations with your teenage daughter. One of the first things you should think about is where you would like to have the conversation. Choose a quiet place where there is privacy for you to talk to your child. For instance, one evening after supper, you could take a quiet walk in the park together. Having a conversation away from the home is a good idea as it will give your teenager a chance to open up and talk about their feelings, without having other family members listening in on the conversation. This conversation should occur in person, and not over the phone or via video calls. Your child should be able to feel safe and comfortable around you, so doing this in person is the best idea. Some parents are far away from their kids because of personal reasons such as work, but this conversation will not go the way you hoped it would if you did it through the phone.

If your teenager doesn't feel comfortable talking to you about the issues they are going through, offer them a list of professionals that might be able to help them. She might prefer talking about it with a therapist, or maybe she would like to speak to someone who is close to her, like a teacher or a family member. Whatever the situation may be, make sure that your teenager is comfortable having this conversation, or else it would bear no fruit in the long run. Think about how you are going to react to any information that your teenager shares with you. Plan out your responses and always think about the bigger picture. You can carry out a small brainstorming session before you start the conversation. Write down the important points that need to be addressed during the conversation, and include ways that you will bring up these points without upsetting your teenager.

Ask Your Teenager How She Feels About Suicide

Asking your teenager what their feelings are with regard to suicide can be terrifying. This is a direct question that can be very uncomfortable for parents to ask their children because they aren't ready to hear their answers. The reality is that more and more teenagers are becoming familiar with suicidal thoughts because of the depression they are facing. Parents wouldn't know this because it isn't something your teenager would just go around talking about. However, when you decide to have a conversation with your child, you have to prepare yourself to hear the good and the bad. If your teenager had to say to you she has been thinking about ending her own life because she cannot handle the pressure of school or family life, what would you say to her? How would you react to her saying those things?

Your reaction means a lot. So whether you agree or not, you have to maintain a calm composure. Some parents might be clueless about the types of questions they should ask their teenagers. You don't want to come across as sounding judgmental or cold towards your teenager, even though you have their best interest at heart. Here are a few examples of the questions you can ask your teenager.

- How much do you know about depression and suicide?
- Where did you learn about depression and suicide?
- Have you ever felt intense feelings of sadness and despair?
- Have you thought about ending your life because you were unhappy?
- Do you feel you can't speak to us, your parents, about your feelings?
- Is there anything we can do to help you? Or do you feel hopeless about the future?

These are some questions you could ask your teenager to figure out how they are feeling. Teenagers are hesitant, so it will take a lot of convincing to get them to open up. However, if you are patient and supportive, it shows your teenager they are not alone and that they can come to you for help anytime. The important thing to remember is your teenager should not feel forced to answer your questions. It must come across as a mutual discussion, without any pressure or coercion from parents. All it takes is one time for you to mess up, and your child may never confide in you again, so please be cautious and supportive during the conversation.

Actively Listen and Understand

During the conversation, your teenager might open up about serious issues that have been causing them pain and making life unbearable. Some of these issues could be related to sex, drugs, alcohol, abuse, family issues, or bullying. When a parent hears their child has been involved in any of the above-mentioned situations, their first reaction would be shock and anger. The shock comes from the fact that you weren't aware of what was going on with your child, and the anger comes from feeling betrayed by your teenager or by a third party who has caused hardship for your child. Whatever the situation may be, it's important that you listen without expressing anger or passing judgment. At this moment, all your teenager needs is someone to listen to what has been going on with them. They are not looking for punishment or judgment from anyone. All they need is to be heard and understood.

That's what you should do as a parent. Actively listen to everything your teenager is saying to you. Take in all the facts, ask questions to gain more clarity into the situation, and respond to your child by either nodding your head or maintaining eye contact. This shows your teenager you are listening to them and you are not lost in your own feelings of anger. Show your teenager you understand what they are feeling. Tell them you understand their position and what they are going through. It doesn't take much to show you care to ensure that they are fully aware of this.

What Should You Do if Your Teenager is Suicidal?

Once you have spoken with your daughter, you should have a clear understanding of how her state of mind is. If you have found that your daughter is suicidal, you have to act fast. Each minute that goes by is painful for your daughter, and now that she has opened up to you, she depends on you for help and support to get through this. It is well understood that parents also feel confused and deeply disturbed at this point. All you might think about is how to stop this pain that your child is experiencing immediately. However, situations like this should be worked through patiently. You cannot rush a solution as it can cause more damage. Below, we have advice on how to go about helping your teenager through this difficult phase. You can navigate through it to prepare yourself to do what is best for your child.

Spend More Time With Your Child

When a teenager is suicidal, they need to be around people who love them. It's important you set aside time daily to spend with your teenager. I understand that it's hard to convince them to spend some time with you, especially since teenagers love to stay in their room all day, but family time is important. You don't have to go out of your way, watching a movie, or baking some cupcakes are great ways to spend time together. The more time you spend together, the closer you will become. This will also help you keep an eye out for suicidal behavior, which would be difficult to do if you weren't spending a lot of time with your teenager. It doesn't matter how old your teenager gets, they still need one-on-one time with their parents. Parents are the backbone of every family—without them around, everything falls apart.

Consider Therapy or Counseling

Seeking professional help is a must when it comes to helping your child overcome suicidal thoughts. There are trained professionals out there who have the ability to help your child. Depression isn't the type of illness that can be cured overnight by taking a few pills. Healing is a process that takes time, especially when there has been a vast amount of damage caused. Set up therapy sessions for your child. Most teenagers won't agree to go to therapy because they are afraid their friends will label them as crazy. It is your job, as a parent, to convince your child that therapy is one of the most effective methods used to overcome depression and suicidal thoughts. Just because you go to therapy doesn't mean you are mentally ill. It is something to be proud of, since you are seeking help to learn how to become better at processing your emotions and understanding those of others. Parents should explain this to their teenagers.

Keep Your Teenager Busy

The more time your teenager has on their hands, the more they will start to overthink. When this happens, a bunch of different emotions show up, making it difficult for them to regulate their feelings. That's how people end up committing suicide—because of overthinking situations and not seeing the bigger picture. As a parent, you should come up with activities to help your teenager stay occupied throughout the day. There are plenty of exciting things you can do to spend time with your teenager.

- Create a list of chores for your teenager to complete daily. Cleaning up their room, washing up the dishes, folding the laundry, these are a few examples of chores that would keep them busy.

- Get your teenager involved with extracurricular activities, such as swimming, martial arts training,cooking classes, or painting. Anything that can calm them down and help them get rid of some steam is beneficial to their recovery from depression.

- Encourage your teenager to get involved in school more often. She can take part in sporting events, fundraisers, and competitions.

- Sign your teenager up to be a volunteer at the retirement home, or at the children's hospital. Helping others will make them feel good, and they will appreciate what they have in life as well.

Encourage Your Teenager to Get in Touch With Their Spiritual Side

If you and your family believe in God, it would be a good idea to encourage your teenager to pursue prayer. Spiritualism has the ability to help people overcome their fears and sorrows by seeking strength and hope from God above. Whether you visit a church, temple, mosque, or synagogue, spending time in prayer will help your teenager let go of the pain and allow God to help her heal and recover. There is nothing to lose from building a personal relationship with God where you can leave all of your cares and worries at his feet. There are millions of people who don't pray or believe that there is a God out there. But for those who do believe, their faith works wonders for their peace of mind and for their overall wellbeing.

Build a Support System for Yourself

As a parent, it's clear you have a lot on your plate. Being there, as a beacon of strength and support, for your child has to be extremely challenging. You are probably dealing with your own sea of emotions that overwhelms you daily. It is crucial you build your own support system to help you cope with it all. You cannot keep it all inside. Sooner or later, you will have a mental breakdown if you bottle up all of your feelings continuously. Talking to someone about your situation will make you feel so much better. If you don't want to talk to your friends and family, you should consider visiting a therapist. If you neglect yourself and overlook the feelings you are experiencing, it will destroy you in the long run. You cannot be strong enough to take care of your child if you don't take care of yourself first. There are things you need as well, such as support, a shoulder to cry on, or someone who can give you good advice.

In Closing

When your teenager is going through depression, it will be difficult for her to come to you and pour her heart out. She may want to hide her feelings for a number of reasons. Maybe she doesn't want to cause you to worry or stress about her, or maybe she is hiding something that has to do with the reason she is depressed. There is no way to tell for sure what your teenager is going through. That is why it is vital for parents to sit down and have a heart-to-heart conversation with their teenagers. Depression can change a person, so much so that their family and friends wouldn't be able to recognize them anymore. Parents have to educate their children on depression and suicide so they will be able to identify the signs in themselves. Most of the time, teenagers don't even realize what's going on inside them. They have no knowledge of what depression is, so they don't understand how fast it can get worse. Be a parent who is not afraid to open their teenager's eyes to the good and the bad side of life.

Chapter 5:

The Importance of Decision-Making

Teaching Your Child How to Make Good Choices in Life

Every day, we are faced with the responsibility of making good decisions for our lives and for those around us. It isn't easy, especially when it comes to making decisions that affect your future. Back when you were a teenager, you may have made a few bad decisions which you look back on and regret today. Take a few minutes to think back on the choices you made. What influenced the way you made decisions back then? Would you have listened to your parents if they advised you against certain decisions? What have you learned from those experiences? Taking your answers into consideration, you will have a better understanding of where your teenage daughter is at with her decision-making skills. In this chapter, we focus on helping you become more involved in the role of a parent. By the end of this chapter, you should be able to educate and guide your child in the way they make decisions.

Why Can't Teenagers Make Good Choices?

Teenagers are the epitome of bad choices. They make poor decisions all the time, and it always gets them into trouble. It's like no matter how many times you advise them to do the right thing, they always manage to make the wrong choices. Some people would say that it's okay to make mistakes, especially when you are a teenager, and to a certain degree, this may be true. However, there comes a time when these mistakes happen regularly and they get overlooked. When this happens, it causes enough damage to have a direct effect on their future. But why do teenagers make stupid decisions? We explore this in more detail below.

Teenagers Aren't Mature Enough

As you are probably aware by now, your teenager's brain hasn't fully developed yet. From childhood through adolescence, up until adulthood, the teenage brain is continuously growing and developing. Your teenager is learning how to deal with different situations every day, and she is learning how to regulate her emotions when things get out of hand. The decisions that she makes during this time won't always be right. Sometimes she will mess up and make choices she will regret later on, and there is no way for her to know whether her decisions are right or wrong when she is in the process of making them. The frontal part of the brain is responsible for decision-making in human beings. Because the teenage brain is still developing, it is difficult for your teenager to comprehend the situation well enough to make the right decisions. Their maturity levels are not on par with those of an adult, so it would be unrealistic to expect them to always make the right choices. You wouldn't expect a 5-year-old child to choose the right type of friends for herself, because she is too young to make that kind of determination. Similarly, you cannot expect your teenager to think like an adult, especially when she doesn't have the support or guidance of her parents.

As the years go by, your teenager will make mistakes and learn from them. These mistakes will open up her eyes, and they will show her what choices to make next time. A human being can only learn through making mistakes. No one automatically knows which decision is the right decision, you have to take a chance and learn from bad decisions. Parents have been there and done that. They can help their teenagers make good choices. But it's easier said than done. There are a lot of teenagers who refuse to listen to their parents or teachers. In this case, the mistakes are theirs to make, and parents can only hope their children learn from the bad decisions they make. Wisdom comes with experience. As your teenager matures, their decision-making skills will become sharper. They will learn more about life as the years go by, and this will help them make decisions that will benefit their future and uplift them in the long run.

Outside Pressure

Teenagers are constantly surrounded by friends and peers. Even though your teenager might have a good understanding of right and wrong, when they are influenced by peers, their decision-making abilities become swayed. For instance, your teenager knows that smoking cigarettes and drinking alcohol on school premises is not allowed, but when they see their friends doing it, they immediately choose to take part. Their friends might directly pressure them into making poor choices, or they might watch their friends doing things they aren't supposed to be doing, and desire to be as cool as them, so they make these poor choices out of their own will. We have discussed direct pressure and indirect pressure in the section on peer pressure. Decisions made because of outside influence always have negative consequences in the long run. Teenagers don't understand that decisions made by others don't necessarily have the same outcome as decisions made by them, and this is where the trouble sets in.

They Refuse Guidance From Others

Try telling a teenager what to do, and see what their reaction would be. They just hate the idea of being told what is right and what is wrong. When someone tries to guide them or tries to help them make a right decision, they take it the wrong way—as if they are being bossed around and undermined by others. Parents will offer the best advice to their teenagers, but it may be ignored because teenagers feel like they are always right. They want to do whatever they like, refuse to be corrected, think they have all the answers to every problem in life, and they feel as if they are never wrong. This is where parents struggle to get their children to listen and take guidance from them. Whenever they try to talk to their teenagers, they are turned down and ignored completely. You, as a parent, might be able to see where your teenager is going wrong. So you naturally offer your advice and ask them to reconsider their choices because you can see they are making a mistake. But your teenager won't listen to you, and she would prefer doing things her own way. They don't even realize the guidance and wisdom they can inherit from their family is something that can help them beat any situation.

Consequences Of Bad Decision-Making

Teenagers often make poor choices in the heat of the moment. They don't stop to think about how these decisions will affect their lives in the present or in the future. In fact, when they are making decisions, they never think about the consequences, or how their actions will affect their lives and the lives of those around them. At that point, decisions are just decisions, and they either chose the right one or the wrong one. As much as we would love to make decisions and have zero consequences attached to them, unfortunately, this isn't possible. Every action has a reaction, and every bad choice has a consequence. Parents must teach their children about how making bad decisions not only affects them in the present but also how it can destroy their future. Here are some consequences that arise from making poor choices in life. Use them to educate your teenager so she can be wary of her actions.

Bad Choices Can Affect Your Health

Saying yes to that line of cocaine, or going out to that nightclub even though they are underage, are examples of what poor choices teenagers make these days. Yes, that type of lifestyle might seem very cool and fun, but there is a certain age for everything. There are valid reasons the government imposes age restrictions on cigarettes and alcohol. You must be 18 years of age and older, if you want to consume alcohol and smoke cigarettes. Why do you think they don't allow anyone below the age of 18 or 21 to consume these substances? A good reason would be that teenagers aged below 18 are still growing and developing. Consuming these substances could adversely affect their brain development and also put their safety in danger. Engaging in substance abuse from a young age could result in illnesses such as cancer, liver disease, heart problems, and brain damage. Engaging in sex from an early age could put you at risk for developing sexually transmitted diseases and falling pregnant at a young age. Parents need to know how to present information like this to their teenagers. You don't want to sound as if you are nagging your child, or as if you are being bossy and telling them what to do. Explain to your child how their spur of the moment bad decision-making could cause major health issues that could last their whole life. If you can, show your teenager videos and other forms of visuals to help them grasp the severity of the situation.

Bad Choices Can Affect Your Career

Teenagers must be made aware of how their bad choices can impact their future careers. Parents have the responsibility to educate their children, and make them aware of how their actions have dire consequences. When your teenager loses focus in their school work, because of the influence of friends, it can derail their plans they have set in motion for their future. The smallest of actions, such as shoplifting with a bunch of friends after school on a Friday afternoon, or being violent with another student at school, could land them in big trouble. Hanging out with people who have drugs in their possession, or keeping drugs on themselves, could place your teenager at risk of being arrested and thrown behind bars. Having a rap sheet isn't good when you are searching for a job, or applying for college. If your teenager is serious about her future, she should be made aware of how her actions and poor decisions could cost her big time.

Bad Choices Could Leave You Spending Your Whole Life Trying to Escape From Them

While not all bad choices have a long-term effect, there are some that can change your life in the blink of an eye. Teenagers around the world have made decisions that have changed their lives completely. They share their experiences on social media to help other teenagers so they don't make the same mistakes. There have been teenagers who got involved in accidents because of drunk driving, and became paralyzed for the rest of their lives. Some had unprotected sex and contracted HIV/Aids, which they are still fighting against today. These are just a few examples of how one stupid decision could leave you repenting for the rest of your life.

If you would ask these teenagers what could have been done to prevent this from happening, they would tell you they wished someone would have educated them and helped them make the right decisions. Others would tell you they wish they had listened to their parents. At the end of the day, all a parent can do is teach their child right from wrong. It's up to the child to make the right decisions. However, the more convincing you are, the greater the chance of your child heeding your advice.

Bad Decisions Cause You to Lose Friends and Family

When you continuously make the wrong decisions, despite the advice and guidance provided by friends and family, you risk losing the relationships that are important to you. The same applies to a teenager who refuses to listen to their parents. When a parent corrects their child and helps them get back up after making mistakes, they expect their child to listen and do better the next time. But when their child ignores warning and carries on making bad decisions, it makes a parent want to step back and remove themselves from the situation.

Eventually, a teenager loses the support and guidance of their parents because of their stubbornness and ego. For instance, a teenager who comes home intoxicated every night, despite the advice and rules laid down by the parents, risks his place in the home and his relationship with his family. The parent reaches their limit and cuts their child out. Friends and family stop coming around because of the poor decisions that a teenager makes, and eventually all contact comes to a standstill. No parent or friend wants to stick around and watch someone they love repeatedly make bad choices. Everyone makes mistakes. Everyone has made poor choices in their lives. Parents should share one of their experiences with their teenagers whilst talking to them about decision making. It will help them see you have also messed up in life, but you have the wisdom to make the right choices thereafter, and learn from your mistakes. You can bond with your child by showing them a vulnerable side of yourself. When parents act perfect in front of their kids, it pushes your kids further away. Your teenager wants to know that you also understand what it's like being that age and making mistakes.

Good Decision-Making Tips for You to Share With Your Teenager

Guiding your teenager doesn't only include giving advice and sharing experiences. It also involves giving them the tools they need to become better people. Now that you have explained how important it is not to make poor choices, you should also provide your teenager with a few useful tips to help them make better decisions in the future. Below, we have listed a few tips you can share with your teenager.

- Don't make decisions when you are stressed. When the pressure is on, and you have to make a decision about something, stress is one of the first emotions that show up—along with frustration and anxiety. When you make decisions under stress and anxiety, you will most likely regret them later on. Your frame of mind is different when put under pressure, so try to take a few deep breaths before you make any decisions, and wait until your mind is clear and free from stress.

- Don't rush into a decision. Rushed decision-making has dire consequences that could stay with you for the rest of your life. Take some time to think about the pros and cons before you rush into anything on the basis of excitement or from outside pressure. If it is a decision that requires an immediate response, remove yourself from the situation for a few minutes, and allow yourself to think without listening to others. A few minutes on your own is all you need to think clearly and make good decisions.

- Don't forget about your values. Whenever you make a decision, always keep your values in mind. Going against your principles and values will guarantee your unhappiness in this decision. No matter what happens, we must always stay true to who we are and what we believe in. Decisions that are made in line with your core values are always the best decisions to make in the end.

- Think about the outcome. Before you make any decisions, think about the outcome first. How will your decisions affect the surrounding people? Are you the only person who will benefit from these decisions? What will the outcome look like? Asking yourself these questions will help you think about the consequences of your decisions in the long run. Most people don't stop to think about this, and that is where they run into trouble.

- Seek advice from a parent or teacher. Decision-making can be difficult for teenagers, especially when they have no one to talk to. Asking a parent or teacher for some advice on a certain decision that they have to make is a good idea. Adults have enough experience to guide the teenager into making good decisions. It's always better to have someone to talk to and seek advice from when things get tough and confusing.

- Weigh out all your options first. Before you make your mind up, weigh out all of your options. Think about the other choices you have, and how things would work out if you decided to make those choices. Which decision benefits you the most? Will this decision be good for your future? Is it really necessary to make this decision? Once you have investigated the different choices you have, go with the one that makes more sense to you. Don't choose out of fear or to make someone else happy.

In Closing

The skills that parents can teach their teenagers about effective decision-making will stay with them for the rest of their lives. It is one of the most valuable lessons a parent can teach their child—as decisions have to be made every day. Even the smallest of decisions can impact the rest of your teenager's life, so it is important to make your teenager aware of this. The more understanding they develop towards decision-making and how it affects the future, the wiser they will become in their decision-making. Although you cannot make decisions for your child, you can be there to support them and give them advice when they need it the most.

Chapter 6:
The Toxic Social Culture of the World Today

Preparing Your Teenager to Face the World

The world is changing constantly. Every day, something new is invented and unleashed into the world. Parents have the responsibility to prepare their teenagers to face the world, so they don't become easy prey for all those horrible people out there. As stubborn as a teenager can be, they have to learn about how the world works and what they need to do to survive out there. In this chapter, we focus on helping parents prepare their teenagers for what's to come.

Youth Culture Today

The youth culture of today heavily relies on technology and social media. Every corner you turn, you will find teenagers buried in their phones all day. From the time they were children, they have been introduced to various forms of technology. By the time they have reached adolescence, they already own their own smart devices, which entertain them constantly. This trend is growing speedily and it is taking over every aspect of our lives. Whilst technology has opened up so many doors for people around the world, and changed so many lives for the better, it has also brought a lot of negativity with it. Youth culture is always changing and evolving, so parents have to ensure they are doing everything they can to prepare their teenagers. Below, we take a look at the different aspects that make up the youth culture of today.

Social Media and its Influence Over Teenage Girls

Social media has grown significantly over the years. Every application we use today are all online based applications. The internet is a place where people from around the world can interact with each other. It doesn't matter if you are living all the way in Sweden, and your friends and family are in America. Social media can bring people together, despite their location, their race, their age, or their financial situation. Teenagers particularly love social media. They enjoy posting pictures, sharing snippets from their personal lives, connecting with friends and family, following celebrities, and much more. There's so much to do on social media, which explains why teenagers are always glued to their devices.

When it comes to teenage girls, social media can become a very dark place. Parents don't always have access to their kids' social media accounts, so it's difficult for them to have an idea of what's going on. People from around the world are able to create accounts on various social media applications and this puts your teenage daughter at risk. There have been multiple cases where girls have been tricked by strangers and fell victim to human trafficking. These people scout through social media to find vulnerable young girls who are easy to trap. That is why it's so important teenage girls don't put out their personal information on social media.

Personal information such as an address, cell numbers, name of school or college, social security numbers, and pictures of their cars with the registration visible. Anyone can access this information and use that to their advantage. Parents must educate their teenage daughters and make them aware of how small mistakes could result in big problems. Apart from the danger and risk to a teenager's life, social media is also used by others as a form of online bullying. Girls use social media to poke fun at other girls, and this has a much deeper impact on the self-confidence of the girls that are being bullied. Once parents are able to make their children wiser about social media, there will be less to worry about. Knowing your teenager is aware of the dangers of sharing too much on social media will help you give them the space they need.

Fashion, Beauty, Celebrities

Another famous trend, which makes up a part of the youth culture today, is the world of fashion and beauty. Teenage girls are drawn towards anything that has to do with fashion. From a young age, girls will flip through fashion magazines in awe of what they see. The glamor, the fame, and the beauty, sucks them in and plants seeds of desire into their little hearts. One day, these girls hope to be just like these models they see posing for these magazines. They want the perfect body, flawless skin, and silky smooth hair, and they are willing to do anything to make themselves look exactly the same as those models. Teenage girls are very impressionable, so if they see something that appeals to them, they are going to pursue it wholeheartedly. The sad thing about it is these teenage girls don't even know what's true and what's fake.

They are misled by the fashion industry into believing that if you have a certain type of figure, then you will be considered beautiful by the world. This toxic culture embeds negativity into every teenage girl, causing them to feel insecure about themselves. It becomes dangerous when teenagers stop eating just so they can achieve that super skinny figure. Adolescent girls are still growing, and their bodies haven't fully reached the point of maturity it's supposed to yet. Good nutrition is important during this stage, as missing out on meals and losing too much weight can affect their menstrual cycle as well. On the other hand, there are a lot of girls who refuse to look skinny. They want to have large breasts and a huge behind, similar to what they see in music videos. There are so many celebrities who boast their curvaceous figures that are in no way natural. Most of these celebs have gained their figures by undergoing breast enhancement surgeries and butt lift injections.

As a parent, learning that your teenage daughter went behind your back and got butt injections is terrifying. When it comes to your child's health, you should be aware of every decision they make. The only way you can avoid this situation is if you are open with your teenager and talk to them about their insecurities. Help them understand how dangerous it is to undergo any cosmetic surgery. If they are hell-bent on changing their physical appearance, reassure them that there is enough time to do that in the future, and explain to them they should have a significant amount of money to get these surgeries done the right way by professionals. This information will help your teenager make a wise decision. If you hadn't been open with them about this, they would have probably gone behind your back and messed up their body at these cheap back door clinics. The more a parent shares the horrors of society with their children, the more power they are giving them to make good choices.

Food and Dieting

Food has changed drastically over the past decade. From being vegan to becoming pescatarian, there are so many variations of being vegetarian nowadays. You would be surprised at how many people like to eat certain types of foods only. Some prefer living off fruits and nuts, others prefer eating vegetables and bread. It's shocking how food has changed and most people enjoy following a strict diet because it helps them stay in shape and be healthy. One of the fastest growing forms of vegetarianism, known as being vegan, is popular among the teenagers of today. When someone identifies as being vegan, it simply means that they do not consume any form of animal products. No eating cheese, milk, eggs, butter, etc. This is a difficult way to live life, especially since all the things we enjoy eating are made of animal products. However, nowadays, teenagers prefer to eat clean and healthy. This can be a great thing if your teenager finds a balance that is perfect for her body.

There are teenagers who take certain diets too far. There are certain ways of doing particular diets. You cannot just jump into a diet without having a clear understanding of what that diet is going to do to your body. For instance, intermittent fasting is a type of diet that restricts you from eating anything between the hours of 6 am till 1 pm. Some teenagers are so desperate to fit into this new culture that they fail to think about their health. Without the proper guidance, these diets could affect your health adversely. Because there are different body types, not all diets will work out. What helped another person lose weight might not work for your teenager, since her body is still changing and developing. Parents must be honest with their daughters about the skewed views of society and be attentive to their actions. If your teenager wants to become involved in a diet plan, support her and encourage her to do so, only if it is for the betterment of her health and wellbeing. She shouldn't consider changing her diet just because her friends are doing it, or because it's a popular way of living. Eating healthy is part of the youth culture, but so is eating sugary, fatty, and oily foods. Parents should teach their child good eating habits, that also involve cheat days for junk foods. Finding a balance is extremely important.

In Closing

This world has a toxic culture that can easily influence millions of teenage girls in many ways. We have mentioned a few aspects where teenage girls become easily swayed because of their interests in fashion, food, and social media. As long as parents are there to guide their children and offer advice on these various aspects, then there is a good chance these teenage girls won't fall prey to these tricks. Your child must understand that what they see on social media and on TV is far from perfect, even though it is portrayed as cool and in demand.

Chapter 7:

The Importance of Self-Respect and Confidence in Adolescence

Teaching Your Daughter How to Be Confident and Respectful.

Every teenage girl has to learn about self-respect and self-confidence. It is, without a doubt, one of the most important things a parent can teach their child. How your teenager looks at herself today will impact how she sees herself in the future. Understanding her true worth is extremely important for your daughter because the world is filled with people who are ready to bring her down and take advantage of her to get what they want. I know that there are some parents who are reading this right now, thinking back to their teenage years. You're probably wondering where your life would be today, if only you believed in yourself back then. Within those thoughts, you are also telling yourself that you will never allow your daughter to make the same mistakes you did. In this chapter, we encourage you to guide your teenager and help them understand their own self-worth.

What is Self-Confidence, and What is Meant By Self-Respect?

Self-confidence is an important part of an individual's life. There are so many people out there who don't understand what self-confidence is, and this holds them back from being the best they can be. Adolescence is a challenging time for teenagers as their bodies are changing constantly. Their physical appearance is changing, their personality is changing, and their intelligence is changing. This is a lot of change to cope with, and it's hard to love yourself when you look in the mirror and don't see perfection. A teenage girl's view of perfection is far from what perfection really is. When they look into the mirror, they don't want to see those red, swollen acne spots on their face. They don't want to look down at their tummy and see a kangaroo pouch bulging through their jeans. When they smile at themselves, they don't want to see their mismatched, crooked teeth.

These things affect their ability to love themselves unconditionally. This is where they lose all confidence in themselves, without even realizing it. Self-confidence is the ability to see all of your flaws and weaknesses and still love yourself unconditionally. While this is easier said than done, it takes a lot of courage to be self-confident. There are a lot of different things that cause a teenage girl to lose confidence in herself. Below, we take a look at the most common reasons girls lose their self-confidence.

How is Confidence Lost?

Growing Up in a Toxic Environment

Being raised in an environment where the people are violent, aggressive, insulting, and abusive has a major impact on the self-confidence of teenage girls. When they are exposed to these traumatizing events from a young age, it robs them of their happiness and excitement that comes with childhood. Parents who verbally and physically abuse their children do so with the intention of hurting them. Telling them they are not good enough, or always pointing out their mistakes instead of praising their successes, are ways that parents put their children down and make them feel inferior. You would think a little constructive criticism would help your teenager pull up their socks and do better next time, and to a certain extent, it works. However, when parents constantly criticize their children, the insults become embedded into the minds of these children where it remains with them throughout life.

A toxic environment also involves one that is abusive in nature. Whether it's sexual abuse, emotional abuse, or physical abuse, it causes a great dent in the self-confidence of a teenager. Being around people who don't value their worth, these teenagers become withdrawn from the world. They no longer have the confidence they need to go out there and socialize with people. These teens cannot try again after failing in their studies at school because they don't believe in themselves. They don't have the support behind them, that will help them push further and not give up. When you don't have people who believe in you, it becomes very difficult to have confidence in yourself, and that is exactly how these teenagers feel. The toxicity of their home life spreads through into other areas of their lives and snatches away their confidence to pursue their dreams.

Being Bullied by Other Kids

Bullying is one of the most common reasons teenagers lose confidence in themselves. It's even more damaging if it starts in early childhood, as it can have a long-lasting impact on the future of that individual. When a child bullies another child, it often comes from a place of insecurity. The bully wants to make other kids feel the same pain and low self-confidence that he or she does, so they will go out of their way to make it happen. Using violence, aggression, assertiveness, and fear, the bully manages to bring other kids down to their knees. These victims develop issues with their self-esteem, and after each encounter with the bully, these teenagers become more insecure about themselves. You must realize that these bullies say mean things every day with the sole intention of causing pain and self-hatred in others, and when this goes on for a long period, it causes damage that cannot be easily repaired. Parents can be bullies, classmates and teachers can be bullies, even siblings and other family members can be bullies. It doesn't matter who the bully is, the level of impact is the same. Being disrespected by others, and being treated like you are lower than them, really messes you up inside. This behavior teenagers receive from others leaves them questioning their self-worth. It makes them feel as if they are nothing special, which instantly causes a dent in their self-esteem.

We will encounter bullies at every stage in life. At school, at home, in college, in the workplace, and in the neighborhood you decide to one day live in. Overcoming that first encounter can be very challenging, especially when you don't have support and motivation from those who love you. Teenagers who are being bullied wouldn't open up to their parents about it. They don't want to feel embarrassed, so they hide the truth from their family members. Parents must be on the lookout for the signs that show your teenager is being bullied. Bullies can be stopped, and the damage can be prevented only if the parents take a stand and do something to help their teenagers.

Experiencing a Trauma and Failure

Trauma is life changing. When someone goes through a traumatic experience, the pain sticks with them for the rest of their lives. There are certain types of trauma that have the power to rob an individual of their self-esteem. For instance, getting involved in an accident and parts of your body have been disfigured, that would lead to major issues with a person's confidence in themselves. Also, being abused sexually or physically can also lead to poor self-confidence issues in the majority of these women. Trauma is never easy to live with. Even though months and years have gone by, the memory is still pretty much here. These memories that replay in your mind cause you to develop a low self-esteem in yourself. This is what holds you back from doing everything you wanted to do so far.

The fear of what has happened follows you throughout life, whispering in your ears that you will never be good enough to achieve your dreams. This is exactly how a teenager would feel when she is experiencing issues with self-confidence. As a girl, it is very important to have confidence in every area of life. Great self-confidence empowers her to be a better version of herself every day, and when this has been taken away from her because of the trauma she experienced in her life, it can be difficult to get back to that place. Everyone will go through something traumatic in their lives, but what is important is how we deal with that trauma. Even experiencing failure in a specific area of life can have a negative impact on an individual's self-confidence. Failure is also a form of trauma, as it can have a huge impact on the lives of those who have experienced it. Have you ever failed at something in life? How do you feel about that incident today? Do you still wish you could have done things differently? Are you afraid of trying again? Your teenager would be feeling the same way if she has lost her confidence because of failure. It can be very traumatic, especially if she has tried more than once and failed each time. Accepting failure isn't easy, but it has to be done so life can move forward. No one wants to be stuck in that horrible phase, lamenting on their failures and mistakes with no confidence in themselves to keep trying again and again.

Self-Respect

Ask anyone what their self-respect means to them, and they will tell you how serious they are about maintaining their respect. Self-respect is even more important to women and girls of all ages. Parents must teach their teenage daughters about how important it is to have respect for themselves in this world today. There is no shortage of people who are ready to take advantage of women and disrespect them—come what may. So the new generation must be able to take a stand for themselves and demand respect from those around them. If you hold yourself in high regard, if you recognize your failures and your success, if you love yourself enough to make sure that no one treats you as if you are nothing, then that is known as self-respect. When a teenager understands her worth, she knows how she wants to be treated, and she will make this very clear to others. Self-respect is very important because the way you look at yourself and how you feel about yourself is the key to how much respect you give to yourself.

The way you talk, the way you dress and your overall behavior, is what builds up your self-respect. Most teenagers use their dressing as a way to express what they are feeling inside. Others might not respect that, but your teenager does, and so should you. Parents must educate their teenage daughters on self-respect and what it involves. No matter how wealthy you are in life, or what job title you hold, if you do not treat yourself with respect, no one else will. Teenagers are not mature enough to understand the in-depth meaning of self-respect. Parents should use clear, straight examples when trying to explain this to their teenage daughters. When you respect yourself, you value your time, your opinions, and your hard work. You love yourself enough to know you deserve to be treated well. When we value ourselves, we don't allow anyone else to put us down or make us feel like we are unworthy. We don't stand for disrespect, and we refuse to entertain people who don't see our value.

How to Overcome Shame and Embarrassment

Carrying shame, or being embarrassed about something that was done in the past, is a toxic way of living life. Your teenager cannot carry such a heavy burden as it can destroy her self-confidence and make her lose respect for herself. Parents should help their teenagers understand how mistakes are a part of the past. Explain to your child that no matter what has been said or done, there is nothing that can change things. Making mistakes as a teenager is a normal part of life, and without mistakes, you cannot learn and grow into a responsible adult. There could be a number of things your teenage daughter might feel ashamed of. Maybe she lost her virginity to a boy that didn't value her enough, or maybe she got bullied by a group of mean girls in front of the whole school. Whatever the situation may be, the end result would be the same. Who, better than a parent, can help a teenager through shame? You can help your teenager be her fun-loving self again. Here are a few tips you can share with your teenage daughter.

Journalize Your Emotions

Journaling is an awesome way of expressing your inner thoughts and emotions without having to say a word. Advise your teenager to start journaling as a way of coping with the mixed emotions she may be dealing with. She might not be able to share all the details of her pain with you, so it will be better if she uses a journal to help her find some comfort and relief from holding everything inside. Your teenager can try journaling twice or thrice a week, or she could capture her feelings every night before bed. The best time to journal is when your teenager is alone. It will help her face her inner feelings that she could be bottling up inside. The great thing about journaling is you don't have to write in it every day, and you don't have to write paragraphs. You get to choose how much you want to share, and when you want to do so.

Speak Words of Positivity

A teenager, who is struggling with shame, would always say negative things about themselves. Parents would hear them say things like, "I'm worthless," "I always make mistakes," "I can never do anything right," or "No one wants me." These are words that can bury their self-confidence for good. So when parents notice their teenagers have been saying things like this about themselves, they should pay attention and sit down with their child and have a conversation. Words of negativity are designed to keep you prisoner in your negative thoughts and mindset. The more your daughter doesn't accept that she has an issue going on, the longer it will take for her to heal and move on. She has to start speaking out words of positivity into her own life, and that will manifest and bring her a good outcome. Teach your daughter to say good things about herself like, "I am not my mistakes," "I can do whatever I put my mind to," or "I am special, and I am loved dearly." These positive words make a huge difference in the atmosphere. Your behavior and your mindset will be renewed by speaking positivity into your life.

Forgive Yourself and Let Go

Forgiveness is an important part of healing and moving forward. Unless your teenager doesn't forgive herself for all the mistakes she's made, it would be impossible for her to move on. As a parent, you never want to see your child walking around with a low self-esteem because of a mistake they made. Encourage your daughter to forgive herself and take what she has learned from her experiences, and use them to make wiser choices. She can break free from the shame and the pain. All she has to do is to learn how to forgive herself. If it helps, your teenager can also try seeking forgiveness from those she has hurt or caused pain. It will help her let go of this chapter in her life where she so desperately wants to close the door. Help your teenager understand everyone makes mistakes, some lose their lives because of it, and some gain success. Your teenager has a choice to decide whether she wants to learn from her mistakes and move on, or whether she wants to remain stubborn and risk getting her life back to enjoy.

How You Can Help Build Self-Confidence in Your Teenager

There are plenty of ways you can help your teenage daughter gain back her lost self-confidence. A teenager struggles to find their place in the world, which leaves them feeling insecure about themselves. Below, we have listed some tips to help you get started. The best part about these tips is your teenager won't even know that you are helping them, which is an advantage since most teenagers hate taking help from their parents.

Love Your Teenager No Matter What

Show your child you love them unconditionally. Your love, as a parent, should not be based on their grades, or on the friends they choose, or on what they look like. A parent's love knows no limit, so make sure that you express how much you love your teenager on a regular basis. The more she knows you love her and that you are there for her, the greater the chance of her coming out of that dark place of no self-esteem. Your teenager will make mistakes, however, that doesn't mean you should hate them for it. You can still express your love, even on days when your teenager gets on your last nerve. Unconditional love can boost confidence in people, so try that with your teenager.

Encourage a Growth Mindset in Your Home

Growth is essential to every area of our lives. We are learning and growing every day, so why not share this with your family? Don't embrace an old-fashioned "fixed mindset" in your home. This is the type of mindset that holds people back and cages them to their mistakes. As a modern parent with a brand-new way of thinking, you can encourage a new mindset within your household. Teach your child that no matter what happens, they should never lose confidence in themselves. In every situation and circumstance, your teenager should understand that nothing will hold them back from achieving their goals. Respecting themselves and respecting others is an important part of growth, and this should be reinforced in your home. It's the new era—people mess up, they own their mistakes, and they move on. No more self-loathing and crying like in the olden days. Now, we forgive one another, and we try to do what's best for everyone.

Accept Failure and Rise Above it

Failure is a powerful force that can hold you back from achieving your goals. If your teenager has experienced low self-esteem issues because she had failed in a certain area of her life, then it will take a while before it gains back her lost confidence. As a parent, you can normalize failure in your home. Now, we aren't suggesting you encourage failure. Instead, if any of your kids had to come home with a report card that shows they failed, you should not make a big deal out of it. Tell your child it's okay, and that they should try to do better next time. Work on ways to help you find out where your child went wrong and what can be done to help them improve. Some parents make it seem as if failure is the end of the world. This causes major confidence issues in their children, who go through life thinking that they are not good enough.

Acknowledge their Achievements and Praise them

When your teenager achieves a goal, like winning a baking competition or passing their finals, make sure you don't lose the opportunity to praise them for their achievement. Showing your teenager how proud you are of them boosts their self-confidence. Recognize their good deeds and say something nice to them now and then. Giving your teenager the recognition they deserve builds them up and keeps them motivated to continue working well towards their goals. It will also teach them how to recognize their own accomplishments and reward themselves for their success. A parent who never recognizes their child's achievements, or praises their child when they have achieved their goals, slowly tears down their child's self-confidence and motivation. Parents, remember, your child comes to you first to boast about their achievements. If you cannot be the one to build them up and motivate them, don't be the one who tears them down and makes them feel worthless, either.

Listen More and Talk Less

Listening to your teenager whenever they have something to say plays a huge factor in how well their self-confidence develops. Parents who always take the time to listen to whatever their children have to say are actually showing them they are important and that whatever they have to say matters. This is important because whenever someone tries to shut them up in the future, they can stand their ground and refuse to be silenced. Home is where all the lessons for life are taught. This is the place where your child learns how to carry themselves out in the real world. If you ignore your child and always brush aside their words whenever they try to talk to you, it will instill a fear inside them that holds them back from speaking out their true feelings. They would accept abuse and be afraid to stand up for themselves whenever someone tries to shut them up. So, parents, spend more time listening to your teenager and less time reprimanding them or talking down at them.

Be an Example of Confidence in the Home

Parents are the first role models for their children. Your teenager will look to you for guidance on how to live life and deal with difficult situations, so you have to show them you have confidence in yourself. As parents, everything we do, we have to think of our kids. Even when we want to break down and cry because we had a bad day, we can't do so out of fear that our children will see. However, your child has to see both sides of you. She must see the strong, confident parent who continues to rise even after facing so many struggles, and she must see the parent who takes a moment to express themselves and cry when they cannot carry their burdens much longer. This will show your teenager that life isn't easy. There will be moments when it gets too much to handle, and you might be on the verge of giving up, but it doesn't end there. You can get back up and continue pressing on with confidence in yourself.

In Closing

Confidence is an extremely vital part of a teenager's life. It is well understood that millions of teenagers struggle with self-esteem issues that hold them back from reaching for their goals. This is because of the phase they are going through, where so many changes are taking place at the same time. Physical changes make them question their outward appearance, which weakens their self-esteem. Emotional changes make them question their family, friends, and their future, which creates doubt and fear within themselves. Parents have the responsibility of supporting their teenage daughters when they are going through phases where their self-confidence takes a hit. Love them, and help them gain back their lost confidence, as it is the most important tool in their future success.

Chapter 8:

Spirituality and Beliefs

Talking to Your Teenager About Their Spirituality

In this chapter, we focus on helping parents speak to their teenagers about getting in touch with their spiritual side. This can be a difficult conversation to have, since many teenagers aren't too keen on prayer. They have other interests which are far from anything that has to do with their belief in God or spiritualism. It's important you make religion and spirituality known to your teenager, so they can make up their own minds when it comes to choosing which way they want to go.

Adolescence and Spirituality

Parents often bring their children up following a certain religion they have followed since before their kids were born. I'm sure you must remember those early Sunday mornings where you had dressed your child up and taken her to church with you. Standing in the congregation, singing songs of praise, you must have hoped that your child would follow your beliefs when they grew up. There are hundreds of different religions in the world today. Spirituality could have a number of different meanings to it from a teenager's viewpoint. With all the chaos going on inside their minds, the last thing they might think about is religion or spirituality. However, it's this spirituality that can help them calm the raging thoughts and emotions they are dealing with in adolescence. Parents should have a conversation about spirituality with their teenagers. This might be a conversation they didn't even realize that they needed.

How to Talk to Your Teenager About Spirituality

Teenagers find themselves more connected to everything else other than religion. Music, dancing, drawing, anything that helps them free their mind and express their emotions. So, when it comes to talking to your child about finding peace and purpose in religion, they might not jump at the opportunity to have that conversation with you. At this tender age, they are busy trying to find their place in the world. They are only just figuring out what makes them happy and what makes them mad, what motivates them and what makes them feel alive. This is a lot to deal with, so don't be upset if your teenager seems uninterested or annoyed whenever you mention "God." Because we understand that this can be a difficult conversation, we have listed some important tips below to help you speak to your teenager about spirituality and religion.

Don't Impose Your Views on Your Child

Parents have a common habit of imposing their beliefs and their opinions on their children, no matter what age they might be. Yes, they are your children, and you have every right to raise them the way you see fit. However, when they become teenagers, they start developing their own views of the world. As a parent, you can guide them and teach them about life, but you cannot make decisions for them, that part they have to do on their own. Life is all about making mistakes, learning, and growing. How will your teenager learn if they don't have the opportunity to make their own mistakes? You can share your views, and you can speak about your feelings to your teenager. But don't try to force them into doing something they don't want to do.

Listen to Their Side

During your conversation with your teenager, make it your priority to listen carefully to everything they are sharing with you. Whether you agree with whatever they're saying, you have to show them you are there to listen and understand before you say anything. Your teenager might have questions she needs to be answered by you, and these questions may have caused an obstacle in her faith or spirituality. Take the time to listen to your child, read their body language and facial expressions—these things say a lot about what they are feeling inside.

Be Patient

If your teenager is uncomfortable with having a conversation about spirituality, take a step back and allow them to have their space. It wouldn't be ethical to force the conversation, or to try and talk them into following your beliefs without their full consent. Parents lack patience when it comes to their children making decisions, and the main reason for this is they are scared that their teenagers will make the wrong choices. At the end of the day, you wouldn't want your teenager blaming you for forcing them into something they weren't ready for. So, you have to be patient and trust that they will make the right decisions for themselves. You can have a conversation about spirituality with your teenager whenever they are ready.

Ways that You Can Help Your Teenager Get Closer to God

Becoming closer to God is a goal that takes most people an entire lifetime to achieve. For a teenager, understanding who God is greatly depends on their personality, their background, and their own personal interests. Teenagers experience things differently than adults, so they would have their own ways to get closer to God that are different from those of their parents. In this section, we help you provide ways that could help your teenager build a relationship with God.

Teenagers and their Love Languages

Every teenager is different, and they each have their own love language that speaks to them on a deeper level. It's through these love languages they are able to feel a connection with God. There are different love languages, such as touch, gifts, quality time, acts of kindness and service, or words of affirmation. Parents should be able to understand which language their child feels more connected to, and they can encourage a relationship with God by using one of these love languages to do so. If you are unable to understand your teenager's love language, answer these questions below to help you figure it out.

- Does your daughter respond to others using touch to express herself? Does she always want hugs and cuddles? If so, then her love language could be touch because it's how she understands the world.
- Does your daughter use words to describe how she is feeling? Does she often complain about things that upset her, and does she use words to express herself? If so, then her love language could be words of affirmation.
- Do you find your daughter constantly asking to spend more time with you? Does she beg you to take her for a drive or for a

walk? Does she always accompany you wherever you go? If so, then her love language is quality time.

- Does your daughter love gifts? Does she ask you for a lot of stuff? Is she happy whenever you gift her something? If so, then her love language is gifts.

Once you have determined what your teenager's love language is, the next step would be to communicate with her using her love language. This will help her open her heart and become more receptive to the conversation about spirituality.

Make Reading About Religion Fun

Teenagers get bored easily, so I doubt they would be all excited and eager to read a thousand-page book all about religion. Whether it's the Bible, the Quran, or the Bhagavad Gita, reading these holy books can be a bit boring, to say the least. Nowadays, these holy books have been designed in such a way to grasp the attention of the reader and keep them interested longer. There are applications that can be downloaded onto your teenager's smartphones, and these apps offer daily devotionals, motivational quotes, testimonies, and notes which can help your teenager learn about God in their own way and in their own time.

Play Spiritual Music and Videos

Playing beautiful, spiritual music in your home is a good way of encouraging your teenager to get closer to God. She could be busy on her phone, or making herself something to eat in the kitchen, but she can still hear the words that are being shared through the music. These words bring hope, comfort, and motivation to pursue a spiritual relationship with God. When your teenager hears this, it will ignite a spark in her heart to become more curious about her spirituality. Another great way to teach your child about God is to watch a good movie about religion and spirituality. Parents should try this when their teenagers refuse to have a conversation about God and spirituality.

Be an Example

Parents are natural role models for their children. Your teenager looks to you for guidance on how to handle certain situations in life. When you are having a bad day, how do you handle the stress? When you are feeling hopeless and depressed, where do you seek comfort? Do you turn to God and seek his help throughout your difficult times? Do you pray daily and make God a priority in your home? The best way to teach and encourage your child to build their own relationship with God is by showing them how to. You cannot tell your child to be more spiritual and follow a certain religion when you don't even believe in God yourself. Be an example, and your child will follow suit if it's truly what they want for themselves.

In Closing

Spirituality is an important aspect of life, and every parent wants their child to be grounded in good values and core ethics that are backed up by their beliefs. We want our children to follow our beliefs and build a life on the foundation of these beliefs. However, your teenager is no longer a child who can't form their own opinions and depends on you to make decisions for them. Your daughter is now transitioning into an adult, and she wants to make her own decisions when it comes to her beliefs and spirituality. All you can do is guide her and encourage her to a certain extent. The rest is up to her. You can follow the tips given in this chapter to help you try to teach your child about God. But if they don't show interest, don't force the issue or hold any anger against them because of their decision. Continue to love your child and be an example that she can look to.

Chapter 9:

Goals and Education

Talking to Your Teenager About Goals and the Importance of Education

In this chapter, we aim to help parents talk to their teenage daughters about the importance of having goals and ambitions in life. Most parents don't even realize how important this conversation is, and they often let their children make decisions about their future without being properly educated about their options. Sometimes, parents aren't clued-up with how diverse the world has become, and this limits their horizon when they think about the future of their children. If you, as a parent, understand how many opportunities are out there in the world, you can encourage your child to pursue these as well.

The Importance of Being Educated and Ambitious as a Young Woman

Around the world, there are millions of young girls who do not have access to an education. Despite the improvements in investments and donations, schools have not been built in many of the Third World countries yet. Young girls wander around their villages, with a hope in their hearts that one day they will be able to go to school so they can have a chance at a good future. This is a picture that is all too familiar, and sadly, this is the situation for many girls in America as well. Education is the key that opens the door to a future where women can be whoever they want to be, and that is an important conversation for parents to have with their teenage daughters. Let's take a look at the benefits of being educated in today's world.

Access to Better Jobs

Being educated enables you to land a job that pays well. Your degree or diploma gives you access to jobs that have a higher pay grade. The reason these jobs pay well is that they need people with a particular skill set who are looking to build a career in that field, and this is achieved through being educated. When you study, you are preparing yourself for a particular career you want to be in for the rest of your life. For instance, if you want to be a doctor or a lawyer, you have to study in order to be considered for these careers. Parents must ensure that they explain this to their teenagers, as it is one of the greatest benefits of being educated.

Financial Freedom

Having the freedom to buy anything you want, whenever you want, without being discouraged by the price tag, is one of the best feelings in the world. Education brings you the financial freedom that everyone is looking for today. Apart from enjoying your dream career, you would also be enjoying the benefits of a good salary. As a woman, it is important to be able to earn well. The world heavily revolves around money, and whether you are a materialistic person, you need money to live a comfortable life nowadays. The average person understands what it is like to sacrifice the things they want, just to be able to afford the things they need. No one wants to live life like that, that is why financial freedom is so important. There isn't a parent in this world that would ever want to say no to their child. You would want to give your child the world, and this is only possible if you have money.

Equality

For a woman, being educated gives you the same access to opportunities that men have. Women can become doctors, lawyers, engineers, anything that they want to, as long as they have an education to back them up. In this world, men are always placed above women, and they always get the highest paying jobs and the reputable careers. Women are expected to stay at home, clean, cook, and raise the children. People always underestimate the true value of a woman, and if you want to be respected and treated like an equal, you have to be educated and independent first. Unfortunately, that is how the world works, so parents must explain this fact to their teenage daughters so they can prepare themselves to face the world.

Self-Dependent

It is crucial that every woman is able to depend on themselves, and not on anyone else. When a woman can take care of herself, no one else will be able to take anything away from her. Teach your daughter that she should not depend on her partner for anything in her life. She must make her own money, pay her own bills, and buy herself whatever she wants without asking anyone for anything. Trust is hard to come across nowadays. Even if someone promises you the world, there is no guarantee they are going to give it to you. There are women who are stuck in abusive relationships and loveless marriages because they are financially dependent on their partners. It goes without saying that people change, circumstances change, and no one is ever prepared for what could happen in the blink of an eye. But if you are dependent on yourself, you have less to worry about.

Confident

Confidence is valuable, especially to a young woman who is finding her place in this world. Being educated gives you a level of confidence no one can ever take away from you. The more you learn about the world around you, the wiser you become, and there are many advantages that come with being a confident young woman. As the famous saying goes, knowledge is power, and when you have power, you will be confident enough to use that power. There will be times when you meet a dead end because it's impossible for you to know everything. However, if you still maintain a high level of confidence, you can make the world your oyster, and you can achieve all your goals and dreams.

Use Your Skills to Contribute to Society

As an educated person, you can use your skills to help better the surrounding community. Poverty and inequality are major problems that plague our society, and our only hope of change lies with those who rise above poverty and inequality. Your community depends on you to use your education to help others. For instance, you spent a number of years studying to become a teacher or a nurse. You can use that education and training to help the people in your community. As a teacher, you could offer lessons free of charge to the underprivileged kids in your area. As a nurse, you could offer monthly BP and diabetes tests to the elderly people in your community. These are just a few examples of how you can help your community through your education. Yes, there are many people out there who do well in life and turn their backs on their community, but you can make a difference and encourage others to pursue an education as well.

Secure the Future

One thing we all look forward to in life is a secure future. There is nothing like waking up every morning, knowing that the future has been taken care of. Without an education, there may be no hope for a bright and secure future. Being educated gives you an advantage that others don't have. You can look into insurance schemes and invest your money for the future. Your education makes you wise and informed about these great opportunities you can use to secure your future. The world is changing and advancing every day, and the only way you can keep up with everyone else is by educating yourself constantly. Women need security in their lives, and they shouldn't have to marry for it. They can secure their own future by being empowered through their education.

Why are Teenagers Unambitious?

Take a few minutes out of your busy schedule and ask a handful of parents how ambitious their teenagers are. Most parents spend a huge part of their time nagging their children about having goals set out for themselves. They feel like their teenage daughters don't have enough drive or ambition in their lives. A large majority of teenage girls spend their time being distracted by fashion, make-up, friends and boys—this is normal for every teenage girl. They just aren't focused enough or motivated enough to think about their careers and their goals. There are a number of reasons why. Let's take a look at a few of these reasons below.

They're Lazy

This is, by far, the most common reason why teenagers are so unambitious. To be completely honest, having goals means you now have something to work towards. Nothing is achieved through daydreaming, as success takes a lot of hard work. Most teenagers don't want to put in the time and effort to achieve their goals, so they decide to just not have any goals to start off with. I think every parent on this planet has called their teenager lazy, at least once. That's just how teenagers are—they shrink away from anything that requires hard work and putting in time. Goals are time-consuming and they require focus and dedication, which is hard for most teenagers. Their preferences, likes and dislikes, and their plans for the future change all the time. They cannot stick to one goal or dream for too long because they become bored and lazy quite fast.

They are Afraid of Change

When a teenager works on goals for themselves, there are certain things that have to change in order to make those goals a reality. Having goals about attending college in another state might be scary for certain teenagers because they don't want to leave their family and friends behind. This is a drastic change that can be scary, so they avoid dreaming about it altogether. This fear of change holds them back from living their lives and doing the things they always want to do. Parents are oblivious to this fear because their teenagers don't talk about it. Life changes all the time, nothing stays the same, and this is what parents need to explain to their children. Goals are a part of life and change is necessary to move forward.

They are Involved in Substance Abuse

Teenagers who become mixed up with drugs and alcohol have zero interest in setting goals for themselves. The only goals they have for their lives are getting high and having fun with their friends. Substance abuse takes over their lives and it completely changes who they are.

The goals and dreams they once had eventually disappear as their personality and rationality disappear over time. These teenagers don't realize their goals could motivate them to get out of this messy situation they're in. The drive and ambition could turn their lives around and their dreams could come true, but it takes a lot of hard work in the process.

They Feel Self Entitled Because They Have Rich Parents

Coming from a wealthy background does play a role in why teenagers have no ambition or goals for their future. They feel as if they don't have to work or build a life for themselves because their parents are wealthy enough to take care of them for the rest of their lives. Just because your parents support you and take care of you doesn't mean they're going to do it forever. No goals, no dreams, no hard work because they can just get whatever they want from their parents. Parents need to be more strict with their teenagers and teach them the importance of goal setting.

Why is Goal-Setting Important?

According to recent studies, it has been found that only 20% of the population sets goals for themselves, and a shocking 92% of these goals are never achieved (*Goal Setting for Teens*, 2016). People never see their goals through. Once life becomes too hectic, they push aside their goals and dreams because there just isn't enough time or resources available to make their goals happen. Parents should help their children learn the importance of setting goals and following through with them. If this is embedded into them from a young age, they will be more persistent in achieving their goals, come what may. Below, we have listed a few reasons why goal setting is important and how you can help your teenager set goals for themselves.

These are Their Goals, Not Yours

The first thing a parent should understand is that these goals are 100% your teenager's and not yours. Before you attempt to help your teenager set goals for themselves, you must make yourself understand that whatever goals your child sets, it's for their own future, and it's based on their happiness and their expectations. You should never try to force your own dreams or goals onto your children. Parents these days tend to force their children into chasing goals and dreams that aren't theirs to begin with. This is where the damage sets in because parents don't realize they are snatching away their child's dreams. It messes your teenager up emotionally and mentally, and this is why they don't end up achieving the goals you set out for them—because it isn't coming from their heart, so they aren't motivated enough to continue pursuing them.

Show them How their Goals are connected to their Happiness

One of the best ways to encourage your teenager to build goals for themselves is to show them how these goals can make them happy in life. Living an authentic life in this day and age can seem impossible, and that is where our happiness comes from. When you set goals for yourself, you are envisioning what you want your life to be like. You are preparing for the ups and downs, and you are making sure you do everything you can to make your dreams a reality. Every time you achieve one of your goals, it will bring an immense amount of happiness into your life. The reward you get after working hard and staying dedicated to your dreams comes in the form of the happiness you feel when you see your dream is now a reality. Parents should explain this to their teenagers so they have a deeper understanding of why goal-setting is so important in our lives.

It Teaches Us How to Dream

Goal setting teaches you how to dream and it fills your heart with hope for a brighter future. Whether your goals are about money, education, family, or health, all of these aspects are important in our lives. When things don't go our way, we often lose hope and close those chapters of our lives. If we failed at something that was important to us, it could have caused us a lot of pain and embarrassment. All hope would be lost and we would be focused on our failures instead of our future. But when we push ourselves to get back up and set new goals for ourselves, it gives life a whole new meaning and brings back hope. We can dream again and look forward to a new happiness in our future.

You Become Responsible and Accountable

The road to achieving goals isn't only about enjoying the rewards. It's also about the lessons you learn along the way. There are many obstacles you will face along the way, and each time you mess up or make any mistakes, you will learn from them and become better. Taking responsibility for your actions and holding yourself accountable for all the mistakes you make enables you to become a wiser individual who can use these experiences to make better decisions in the future. Goal setting will place you under an enormous amount of pressure, and it will mold you to become a better version of yourself. The process will only work if you don't give up and stay committed to your goals. Parents must encourage their children to face their obstacles and fight for their dreams no matter what happens.

In Closing

Goals and education are vital aspects of life that every girl should embrace wholeheartedly. As women, we have spent hundreds of years fighting for our freedom and equality. Even though we have managed to achieve so much over the years, there are still people in this world who look down on us, and they wait for an opportunity to take advantage of our kindness and good nature. Our weapon, our ultimate key to living a confident life, is our education. We can achieve anything we put our mind to, and this is made possible because of our knowledge and experience. Please encourage your daughters to pursue their education and develop meaningful goals for their lives. Your daughters will thank you one day for teaching them how to live life the right way.

Chapter 10:
Conflict Management

Talking to Your teenager About Managing Conflict in a Healthy Way

Conflict is a part of our lives, and it can happen at any time with anyone. We see it on the TV, hear it on the news, and read about it on social media. No matter what we do, there is just no avoiding it, so the best thing we can do is learn to manage it. Teenagers find themselves engulfed with conflict more because of their loose tempers and their emotional immaturity. Fights are common among teenagers and every parent would agree with this statement. You would be especially surprised to learn that teenage girls get into fights more often than boys. In this chapter, we explore the reasons behind increased conflict in a teenager's life, and we highlight important tips to help your teenager deal with conflict positively.

Why are Teenagers Always Involved in Conflict?

Teenagers are often viewed as troubled individuals who are always moody and ready for a fight. It seems like wherever they go, trouble follows them. There are many reasons a teenager could be involved in conflict regularly. Parents often see what is happening on the outside, but never what is happening on the inside. Some teenagers carry around a lot of anger and hurt, and this later manifests when they are faced with difficult situations. In this section, we will explore the main reasons teenagers may be attracting conflict wherever they go.

Family Issues

A teenager's anger issues might very well stem from violence and conflict that has occurred in the home. They must have grown up watching family members fight on a daily basis, and now they probably think conflict is a normal part of life and that is how they should behave with those around them. Being around people who use violence as a way of dealing with conflict paints a disturbing image in a child's mind, and this is how they grow up thinking violence solves conflict. So when they face situations at school or out in public, they immediately resort to violence instead of handling their issues calmly and wisely. Home is where teenagers are exposed to a lot of things that contribute to their overall behavior and mindset.

Trauma

As mentioned previously, trauma can impact a teenager in many ways. One of the major ways that trauma affects a teenager is it causes a tremendous amount of shame and anger. These feelings become bottled up inside and this later results in conflict and violent outbursts. Trauma changes people and it makes an individual look at everyone around them as an enemy. Trust isn't passed out easily, mainly because of the pain and betrayal they have encountered. Teenagers who have been affected by trauma are very sensitive. Even the smallest of disagreements could turn into something big because they take everything so personally—as a direct attack.

Hormones

Raging hormones contribute significantly towards how a teenager deals with their problems. Unfortunately, unstable hormones are part of being a teenager, and there is no way that it can be avoided. It can be managed, however, using the right tools. People always say that teenagers are moody, stubborn people who like things done their way. These hormones are the reason teenagers are always moody—happy one moment and angry the next. Dealing with conflict can seem impossible when a teenager is experiencing all of these different emotions. Every emotion feels more heightened because of these hormonal changes in the body, and the only thing a teenager would want to do is express their feelings, instead of calmly working on a solution to resolve conflict.

Peer Pressure

Conflict also arises as a result of peer pressure among teenagers. When a teenager is constantly being pressured into doing stuff that they are not comfortable with, they will eventually crack under pressure and lash out at those around them. Fights will then break out among the group, resulting in conflict and, in some cases, violence. Parents might think that fights among friends are common, however, it could become more serious when a teenager is being forced to go against their own values. Bullies will also resort to violence when things don't go their way, and teenagers who are being bullied have to deal with this type of conflict on a daily basis.

How Will Poor Conflict Management Impact a Teenager's Life?

Poor conflict management can have a massive impact on a teenager's life in the long run. During adolescence, we develop critical skills that enable us to function as a well-balanced human being in society. We learn how to show compassion, how to deal with real-life problems, how to manage our anger, and how to resolve conflict. Our parents and guardians have the responsibility to teach us about these skills, and to demonstrate in real life how difficult situations should be handled correctly. When we are taught the wrong way to handle difficult situations, it causes chaos in our lives. Your teenager is depending on you to lead them and direct them down the right path. If you don't teach them how to manage conflict, it could affect their lives negatively. Let's take a look at what happens when conflict isn't managed properly during teenage years.

Lack of Control Over Emotions

Poor conflict management could impair your ability to control your emotions during difficult situations. If you cannot manage your behavior during a conflict, how are you going to take control of your emotions? Because of this, you will not be able to control your feelings, which is important in conflict resolution. Letting your emotions run wild, and giving in to anger and aggression, only builds up conflict and feeds it to make it stronger. Grasping the reins over your emotions is very important in situations where potential conflict is a cause for concern. Your teenager's self-regulation abilities are important for their future. Dealing with conflict during their teenage years will prepare them for the future and it will equip them to gain conflict management skills, which are important to help control emotions as well.

Violent Behavior

Being exposed to conflict frequently is a cause for concern among teenagers. If parents allow their teenagers to handle all their problems using violence, it will become the norm even when they become adults. When a teenager becomes violent at a young age, it could potentially become a part of how they handle difficult situations in the future. Using violence to get their way, or using violence to intimidate other people, is the type of behavior and lifestyle that a teenager will embrace once they become adults. If parents don't correct violent behavior during adolescence, then these teenagers will be under the impression that it is okay to use violence on someone else. Violence blows up conflict, and this isn't something that teenagers should be proud of. Hurting other people is not the way to resolve conflict.

Damage to Your Social Life

A person who thrives in conflict becomes someone who eventually loses their friends and family. No one wants to entertain a person in their group who doesn't know how to maintain peace and deal with conflict in a healthy manner. When an issue comes up among friends, it should be dealt with using great conflict management skills. A person who has zero skills when it comes to resolving conflict, will not be able to be a peacemaker in the group, and that is when they start jumping from group to group, trying to find their place and trying to maintain a social life.

Broken relationships

Later on in life, when marriage and kids come along, a person should be able to handle conflict well. There are disagreements in every marriage, and it takes a well grounded individual to handle those problems positively. If your teenager doesn't learn how to manage conflict during their adolescent years, it will ruin their future relationships, without a doubt. What will they teach their kids? Will the cycle continue from parent to child? Hence, it is so crucial that people work on their problem-solving skills as much as they possibly can for the success of their future relationships.

Mental Health Issues

It goes without saying that continuous exposure to conflict has the ability to produce mental health issues in people. Because conflict is so frustrating and exhausting, it can affect a person's frame of mind, causing them to become depressed, anxious, and paranoid. They become depressed because of the broken friendships and relationships that have been lost as a result of constant fighting. They become anxious and paranoid because they are living in fear of when the next problem will come. Since they don't know how to manage conflict, the only thing they can do is live life in fear of getting into another messy situation that they don't know how to handle it. Life becomes miserable for these teenagers, and mental illness is bound to set in when this happens. Being ostracized from groups at school and being avoided by family members makes them feel lonely and unloved.

Ways Your Teenager Can Manage Conflict

Even though conflict is an unavoidable part of our lives, there are ways we can use to manage our response towards it. There are so many benefits to managing conflict, and parents should be open with their teenagers about these benefits, as it could help them understand why conflict management is so important. Here are a few of the benefits that come with conflict management.

- Managing conflict helps reduce stress among the family.
- It strengthens the relationship between parent and child.
- Promotes respect for others, and earns you respect as well.
- Teaches you important skills for life.
- Reduces the risk of mental health issues.
- Reduces violent outbursts during conflict.
- Helps build your personality and attracts people towards you.

As you can see, there are many benefits to learning positive conflict management skills. Parents must understand it can be difficult for teenagers to understand the importance of dealing with conflict correctly. Don't give up on your teenager. Continue to encourage them to use the tips below whenever they are faced with a conflict in their lives. Explain to them you don't expect a change in their behavior overnight, but you do expect them to put in the effort when it comes to conflict resolution and management. Below, we take a look at some of the best conflict management tips that will help your teenager respond to conflict positively.

Tips For Managing Conflict as a Teenager

- Remain calm - When you find yourself in the midst of conflict, the first thing you should do is remain calm. Take a few minutes to gather your thoughts and reframe your mind.

- Respect the other person - Before you say anything out of anger, think about how you would like to be treated. Be respectful about how you respond to the other people who are involved in the conflict.

- Don't attack - Try your best not to attack the other person by saying things that are embarrassing or demeaning. Do not resort to violence or any other form of physical action.

- Explain how you feel - Always try to express how you are feeling, rather than being defensive and rude towards the other person. Once people understand how the conflict is affecting you, they will be able to work with you to resolve it.

- Listen actively - Listen to what the other person is saying and try to understand things from their perspective before you pass out any judgment.

- Avoid conflict if you can - The best way to manage conflict is to try and avoid it. Pick your battles and learn to walk away from situations that don't require your input. If the problem doesn't concern you, stay away from it.

- Show empathy - Think about how the other person is feeling at that moment. Try to put yourself in their shoes. Only then will you be able to calm down and understand. No two people are alike, and we all have our own way of dealing with conflict.

In Closing

Parents, encourage your teenager to practice conflict management whenever she can. Girls are emotional by nature, so it is important they learn how to control their emotions whenever conflict arises. Try to make her understand that poor conflict management could end up ruining her life in a big way. Relationships could fail, friends would leave, even her career could be jeopardized by her inability to control her response towards conflict. As long as you don't judge her or make her feel bad about herself, she will be open to taking your advice on developing conflict management skills. The best thing you can do to help your daughter is to be an example for her to follow.

Conclusion

Your baby girl is growing up faster than you can imagine. She isn't that little girl anymore, who walks around the house in mommy's high-heeled shoes with a fancy purse on her arm. Now, she is a teenager, and raising a teenage daughter is no walk in the park—that I can assure you. There will be days when you will feel so blessed you have a wonderful daughter who is growing into a young woman. And there will be days when you feel like pulling all the hair out of your head because your teenager is too stubborn and rebellious. This responsibility you have been blessed with takes a lot of courage and patience on your part. Teenage girls are cheeky, daring, emotional, and outspoken. They can be very opinionated, which is both a blessing and a curse. As a parent, you only want what's best for your child, and you are willing to do anything to protect her from the wickedness of this world. But it is a tough job, and there will be conversations you need to have with your teenage daughter.

This book has provided you with some great conversation topics that are important for every teenage girl to know about. Topics such as sex, changes in puberty, the importance of making good decisions, being weary of social media, and handling conflict have been highlighted in detail for you to share with your daughter. I know that you have gained the confidence you desperately needed to speak to your child just by reading through this book. The sooner you sit down and have these conversations with your teenager, the better it will be for her own wellbeing. Always remember to be patient and empathetic towards your child. She is going through a confusing time in her life, and she is still learning about her place in the world. Be supportive, be encouraging, but most importantly, show her you love her unconditionally.

References

Decision making 101. (n.d.). Au.reachout.com. https://au.reachout.com/articles/decision-making-101

default - Stanford Children's Health. (2019). Stanfordchildrens.org. https://www.stanfordchildrens.org/en/topic/default?id=puberty-adolescent-female-90-P01635

Divecha, D. (2017, October 20). *How Teens Today Are Different from Past Generations.* Greater Good. https://greatergood.berkeley.edu/article/item/how_teens_today_are_different_from_past_generations

Fulghum, D. (2008, June 4). *Depression Diagnosis.* WebMD; WebMD. https://www.webmd.com/depression/guide/depression-diagnosis

Goal Setting For Teens. (2016, June 7). 7 Mindsets. https://7mindsets.com/smart-goal-setting-for-students/

Help Teens Learn to Control Emotions. (2020, January 3). Center for Parent and Teen Communication. https://parentandteen.com/self-regulation/

How to Help Your Teen Get Closer to God. (2022, March 18). Focus on the Family. https://www.focusonthefamily.com/parenting/how-to-help-your-teen-get-closer-to-god/

May 28, C. P., & 2020. (n.d.). *Ask Your Teen These 20 Questions and You Could Come Out of the Convo Closer.* Parents. Retrieved March 27,

2022, from https://www.parents.com/kids/teens/questions-for-teens-to-help-you-bond/

Mayo Clinic. (2018, November 16). *Teen depression - Symptoms and causes.* Mayo Clinic; Mayo Clinic. https://www.mayoclinic.org/diseases-conditions/teen-depression/symptoms-causes/syc-20350985

McCue, J. (2018, January 22). *A parent's guide to why teens make bad decisions.* The Conversation. https://theconversation.com/a-parents-guide-to-why-teens-make-bad-decisions-88246

Neighmond, P. (2013, December 2). *School Stress Takes A Toll On Health, Teens And Parents Say.* NPR.org; Patti Neighmond. https://www.npr.org/sections/health-shots/2013/12/02/246599742/school-stress-takes-a-toll-on-health-teens-and-parents-say

Peer pressure and teenagers - ReachOut Parents. (2019). Reachout.com. https://parents.au.reachout.com/common-concerns/everyday-issues/peer-pressure-and-teenagers

Peer Pressure: Strategies to Help Teens Handle it Effectively. (2018, September 4). Center for Parent and Teen Communication. https://parentandteen.com/handle-peer-pressure/

Puberty in Girls: What Every Teen Girl Needs to Know. (n.d.). GoodRx. Retrieved March 27, 2022, from https://www.goodrx.com/health-topic/teen-health/puberty-guide-for-girls

Schmidt, S. (2020, February 5). *Modern Culture Of The Youth: Do You Know It Well?* River Beats Dance. https://riverbeats.life/modern-culture-of-the-youth-do-you-know-it-well/#:~:text=Today%2C%20youth%20culture%20is%20impossible

September 10, & Pediatrics, 2021 |. (2013, November 5). *How Peer Pressure Affects Teenagers.* Scripps Health. https://www.scripps.org/news_items/4648-how-does-peer-pressure-affect-a-teen-s-social-development#:~:text=Negative%20peer%20pressure%20can%20lead

Sexually transmitted infections (STIs). (n.d.). Www.who.int. https://www.who.int/news-room/fact-sheets/detail/sexually-transmitted-infections-(stis)#:~:text=Of%20these%2C%204%20are%20currently

Talking with Your Teens about Sex: Going Beyond "the Talk." (2020). https://www.cdc.gov/healthyyouth/protective/factsheets/talking_teens.htm

Teens and Peer Pressure - Children's Health. (2020). Childrens.com. https://www.childrens.com/health-wellness/helping-teens-deal-with-peer-pressure

Image References

Bhiju, A. (2021, March 1). *Teenage girl looking away.* Pexels.com. https://www.pexels.com/photo/teenage-girl-looking-away-7633967/

Bro, C. (2020, March 27). *Person in black jacket and blue denim jeans sitting down.* Pexels.com. https://www.pexels.com/photo/person-in-black-jacket-and-blue-denim-jeans-sitting-on-black-couch-4100655/

Burton, K. (2020a, December 1). *Diverse classmates bullying Hispanic student*. Pexels.com. https://www.pexels.com/photo/diverse-classmates-bullying-hispanic-student-in-university-6147156/

Burton, K. (2020b, December 1). *Multiethnic male students gossiping about sad crying girl*. Pexels.com. https://www.pexels.com/photo/multiethnic-male-students-gossiping-about-sad-crying-wo

Cottonbro. (2020a, October 8). *parent and child talking in the bedroom*. Pexels.com. https://www.pexels.com/photo/man-love-people-woman-6593903/

Cottonbro. (2020b, December 11). *A mother holding condoms while talking to daughter*. Pexels.com. https://www.pexels.com/photo/a-mother-holding-condoms-while-looking-at-the-paper-with-her-daughter-6471421/

Cottonbro. (2021, April 23). *woman sitting on floor*. Pexels.com. https://www.pexels.com/photo/woman-in-white-lingerie-sitting-on-the-floor-8746734/

Grabowska, K. (2021, April 24). *A woman in a pink blazer helping a young girl*. Pexels.com. https://www.pexels.com/photo/a-woman-in-pink-blazer-writing-on-a-notebook-beside-a-young-woman-7692560/

Khan, I. (2015, March 15). *Man in black shirt and grey denim pants*. Pexels.com. https://www.pexels.com/photo/man-in-black-shirt-and-gray-denim-pants-sitting-on-gray-padded-bench-1134204/

Lach, R. (2021, June 30). *A young couple sitting on a lakeshore.* Pexels.com. https://www.pexels.com/photo/a-young-couple-sitting-on-a-lakeshore-9652780/

Lusina, A. (2020, October 26). *Crop man covering mouth of woman.* Pexels.com. https://www.pexels.com/photo/crop-man-covering-mouth-of-woman-5723196/

Matos, T. (2020, May 30). *Woman with smeared eyes in studio.* Pexels.com. https://www.pexels.com/photo/woman-with-smeared-eyes-in-studio-4576085/

Monstera. (2020, February 23). *Diverse woman standing together.* Pexels.com. https://www.pexels.com/photo/diverse-woman-standing-close-and-looking-at-camera-6238119/

Monstera. (2021, March 11). *Faceless people scolding discontent black girl.* Pexels.com. https://www.pexels.com/photo/faceless-people-scolding-discontent-black-girl-7114755/

Nekrashevich, A. (2020, December 2). *Woman applying facial serum.* Pexels.com. https://www.pexels.com/photo/woman-applying-facial-serum-6476077/

Pak, G. (2021, April). *Man and woman holding their diploma.* Pexels.com. https://www.pexels.com/photo/man-and-woman-holding-their-diplomas-7973211/

Piacquadio, A. (2018, April 25). *Young troubled teenager sitting by her laptop.* Pexels.com. https://www.pexels.com/photo/young-troubled-woman-using-laptop-at-home-3755755/

Studio, R. (2020, February 23). *Woman in black top sitting alone.* Pexels.com. https://www.pexels.com/photo/woman-in-black-spaghetti-strap-top-and-black-leggings-3820319/

Summer, L. (2020, December 17). *Irritated woman scolding in the kitchen.* Pexels.com. https://www.pexels.com/photo/irritated-diverse-women-scolding-in-kitchen-6382679/

Von, M. (2018, October 3). *sitting woman wearing white shirt and blue jeans.* Unsplash.com. https://unsplash.com/photos/F4nn2XdyuiI

www.ingramcontent.com/pod-product-compliance
Lightning Source LLC
Chambersburg PA
CBHW010707020526
44107CB00082B/2702